MORE ENGINEERING
PROJECTS FOR YOUNG
SCIENTISTS

PETER H. GOODWIN

MORE ENGINEERING PROJECTS FOR YOUNG SCIENTISTS

FRANKLIN WATTS
NEW YORK | CHICAGO | LONDON | TORONTO | SYDNEY

Photographs copyright ©: The Toro Company, Minneapolis, Minn.: p. 24; Fundamental Photos: pp. 29 (Richard Megna), 63, 68 (both Carla Breeze); Photo Researchers: pp. 35 (Jean-Marc Barey), 46 right (Lowell Georgia), 54 (Alexander Lowry); Mike Kentz, NYC: p. 46 left; Susan Van Etten: p. 71; NOAA: p. 94; Comstock/Russ Kinne: p. 105; Astronomical Society of the Pacific: p. 110.

Library of Congress Cataloging-in-Publication Data

Goodwin, Peter, 1951–
More engineering projects for young scientists / Peter H. Goodwin.
p. cm. — (Projects for young scientists)
Includes bibliographical references and index.
ISBN 0-531-11193-8 (lib. bdg.)
1. Engineering—Experiments—Juvenile literature. 2. Physics—
Experiments—Juvenile literature. [1. Engineering—Experiments.
2. Physics—Experiments. 3. Experiments.] I. Title. II. Series.
TA149.G67 1994
620'.0078—dc20 94-26877 CIP AC

Dedicated to everyone who has an interest in science

CONTENTS

CHAPTER 1
Engineering and Experiments **11**

Chapter 2
Working Scientifically **16**

Chapter 3
Energy **19**
Tire Pressure and Rolling Friction   20
String Trimmers   23
Gears, Bicycles, and Other Things   28
Energy in Rubber Bands and Springs   32
Spinning Basketballs   34
Torque Converters and Automatic Shifts   39
Designing a Rocking Chair   45
Other Projects with Energy   49

Chapter 4
Engineering and the Environment **52**
Windmills   53

Wave Energy 57
A Passive Solar-Heated House 62
Solar Heating 66
Keeping Heat In with Insulation 70
Storing Heat from Solar Collectors 74
Characteristics of Light and the Environment 78
Other Projects with Environmental Engineering 81

Chapter 5
Weather, Robots, and Remote Sensing **84**
Dew Point and Clouds 85
Heating and Cooling with Changes of State 90
Wind Speed Indicators 92
Light-Emitting Diodes (LEDs) and Transistors 98
Robots and Repetitive Tasks 103
Remote Sensing 108
Other Projects with Weather, Robots,
and Remote Sensing 113

Chapter 6
Science Fairs **116**

Bibliography **120**

Index **122**

MORE ENGINEERING
PROJECTS FOR YOUNG
SCIENTISTS

1

ENGINEERING
AND EXPERIMENTS

The word "engineering" may be scary to people who are not familiar with how engineers work or what they do. However, engineering is simply applying what you know to solve a problem.

Engineering is important because it is where science and society meet. Scientists work to understand nature better and society has problems needing to be solved. Engineering applies science to problems. It develops machines or devices that can make life easier, safer, more efficient, or more pollution-free. Many scientific discoveries are made every day. However, these discoveries may be useless unless they can be used to solve problems. Superconducting materials are neat science, gee whiz stuff, but unless society can use these materials or scientists can learn from working with them and then invent other useful things, they are just neat toys. Luckily, engineers can use these superconductors in many areas including medicine. They have engineered the materials into useful things for our society.

This book helps you to think like an engineer. It helps you run experiments and build things. Your experiments may not solve any major problem for the world, but then again, you may discover something that no one else has. Sometimes people who ask "simple" questions or run "simple" experiments find out answers that are very important. It has happened before and will happen again. The ideas for experiments in this book may help you ask the right questions. A "right" question is one that allows you to learn something you didn't know before. It may also be that no one else knew the answer before. If you find the answer, you have really done something.

Engineering involves thinking scientifically and applying scientific principles. It also requires that you know something about how things work. In order to build a tree house, you have to engineer it. You must choose your materials properly. If they are not strong enough, you may find yourself on the ground after falling from some great height. If you build a tree house with materials that are much stronger than you need, you will waste money: It won't be an "efficient" structure. You should also think about how it looks, how practical the rooms are, and how safe the inhabitants will be.

Engineers are rather normal people who generally enjoy their jobs. Imagine spending your time trying to figure out how to do something better or with less money. It is almost like a game, a treasure hunt. Imagine you are one of the engineers who designed the laser system used to check out items at a supermarket. Someone tells you they want a fast, accurate system to identify products by their "bar codes," the dark lines on most products with numbers underneath them. You then apply what you know about lasers, optics, and computers to identify what was being bought. When your system is working properly, it saves time, allows the store to keep track of its inventory, and easily changes the prices of items for sales. If your system works and had been designed efficiently, you could then sell it and make a profit, either for yourself or for your company. If you had designed the system, think of how much fun it would be to see one in action and know that it was your design!

You actually have done quite a bit of engineering in your life. You have probably run experiments with building blocks. As you grew older, you built more complex towers and then knocked them down. You might have also built sand castles at the beach and then tried to engineer ways to protect them from the waves or tides.

We use scientific principles daily so basic engineering comes quite naturally. You may not know all the proper scientific terms, but you can still use the principles. As your observations and experiments become more complex, more precise words may help to describe the things you see. Knowing more about scientific principles may also allow you to be more efficient in your research and may help you to reach better conclusions.

Some engineering experiments require you to use numbers, although the math is often quite easy. You can often draw good conclusions from experiments even if you are not a math whiz. Only a few projects in this book require more than basic math.

As you experiment, realize that engineers rarely find answers immediately. It often takes time to work out solutions. If an experiment doesn't work, try to think about what went wrong. Sometimes a simple, careless mistake can cause large problems. Check to see that everything is in its proper place, have patience, and think about what you are doing.

Experimenting and trying to engineer solutions take courage because sometimes experiments fail and you must pick up the pieces and continue. When the experiment doesn't work, something may have happened that you didn't understand or do correctly. However, failures are often important and may lead to discoveries that are unexpected. Remember, science does not always move along smoothly.

This book helps guide you in the experimental method. It helps you ask questions, get started on a basic experiment, and draw conclusions from your data. Chapters contain related projects with background material to help you understand the experiments. The relationship between science and society is discussed often to show how engineering can help society. Each project has a basic experiment or two and then additional suggestions for further projects. At the end of each chapter, suggestions are given for other experiments related to the topic.

Each project is meant as a starting point and should lead you to new questions. You should not just answer the questions asked in the book; you should ask a few more of your own and investigate them. Some of the basic experiments can be done quickly and are suitable for a classroom science project. Others may take more time during weekends or vacations. While the basic investigations probably are not original enough to win at large science fairs, some project extensions can be used for science fair projects.

Very often, you will have to improvise as you run your experiments. The directions might say you need weights and you don't have any. Well, maybe you could use paper clips or pens or some other things as units of weight. Engineers often do the same thing because they don't have enough money to buy the things they would like. However, if you use materials other than those discussed in the book, check with an adult to see whether they are safe. Safety is important to engineers.

Experimenting in science is fun and may help you understand your world more clearly. You may discover things that are important for you or for those around you. The only thing you need is a desire to learn and find out about new things. Remember, these experiments are just the beginning. The most important experiment you do may result from a question *you* ask: "What would happen if I just did that? Would things work better?"

Now that you have an idea about what you are going to find in this book, it is time to start running experiments. Don't forget to enjoy your work. You might even spend your life running experiments and designing things. We call people who do that engineers. Others run experiments of their own just for fun. They engineer things, too.

2

WORKING SCIENTIFICALLY

Scientists work by asking questions and then trying to find answers to those questions. This is similar to how most people solve problems, but sometimes scientists follow a more formal procedure. The procedure involves developing a hypothesis or statement of what they want to test, getting data, and drawing conclusions.

If you say, "I think the full moon is the same size when it is near the horizon as it is high in the sky," you are stating a hypothesis. A hypothesis is a guess at an answer and may be right or wrong. In order to see whether the hypothesis is correct, you collect data. You might collect approximate data by observing the moon near the horizon and putting your thumb over it when your arm is outstretched as in Figure 1. Repeat your measurement when the moon is high in the sky. You have now collected data you can analyze to conclude whether your hypothesis is correct. It may be that you still are not sure; if so, you can make more precise measurements and collect more data.

Collecting the data to prove or disprove a hypothesis

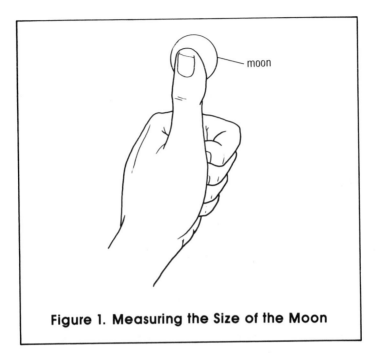

Figure 1. Measuring the Size of the Moon

may be easy or hard. However, the more data you collect, and the more precise the data are, the more certain you will be about your conclusion, the answer to your question.

Investigating the size of the moon is a simple example of what scientists do. Scientists start an investigation because they have questions. "Hey, I wonder if I can make a more efficient solar collector out of this material?" A hypothesis would be "I think this material will collect more heat than other materials." This is a guess at an answer that the scientist then tests with an experiment. He or she would collect data to find which materials collect more heat when the sun is shining. After taking the data, the scientist would make a conclusion based on the data.

Scientists have to make sure that their data are valid. Scientists use controls for this purpose. The control allows you to compare one result with another. If you are testing materials for solar heating, you must be careful that something other than the material you are testing in your experiment isn't causing the differences you observe. Were the collectors you used for comparison the same except for the different collector material? If you change the collector material, you can't change the size, the insulation, or any other variable.

Using a control is very important in scientific work. Many improper conclusions have been drawn because there was no "control" for comparison. As you run your experiments, think about what you change in an experiment. Your data may support your conclusions but for the wrong reasons. The data may literally be telling you the wrong thing.

You must also be careful when you engineer a machine. You must test it completely or it may work in some situations but fall apart in others. If your solar collector works well at one temperature but melts when the temperature rises too much, then your collector isn't useful.

As you run experiments, generally you should follow the scientific method. Develop a hypothesis; plan your experiment carefully, including a control; and run it carefully to collect data. Make careful measurements and record the data in a notebook. Using a notebook is better than jotting notes on pieces of paper because you may lose data. A book keeps the data together. If your data supports your hypothesis, then your hypothesis may be correct. Your data may show the opposite, too.

You should remember that you may never be able to *prove* your solution works in all situations. Some questions may remain unsolved or tested. Einstein made mistakes as he worked, and sometimes his theories did not completely explain the world. There will always be some unanswered questions that others will have to answer.

3

ENERGY

Energy is defined as the ability to do work; work occurs when a force is exerted for a distance. When you ride a bicycle, you exert a force on the pedals, which move—so you do work. In order to do the work, you need energy that comes from food. Food energy allows you to pedal the bicycle.

Heat is one form of energy. Sometimes heat energy keeps things warm, as it does in houses in winter, while other times heat energy does work. Heat energy released by burning gasoline makes most cars go. The heat energy does work, as the engine exerts a force to make the car move forward.

Because energy sources are limited and expensive, saving energy is very important. The United States imports much of the oil it uses, and this is bad for the balance of trade. Burning oil and gas also causes pollution, which affects our country and the rest of the world. Because saving energy is important, engineers try to find more efficient ways to use it and to avoid wasting it.

The experiments in this section will help you understand energy better. While they won't all show you how to save energy, they will give you a better understanding of what energy is. You may also get an idea from one of these experiments that will make you interested in running more experiments. Who knows, you might become an engineer. As you start your investigations, remember to have fun. At times, working on your project may be hard, but engineers have fun, too.

TIRE PRESSURE AND ROLLING FRICTION

Whether you are driving a car or riding a bicycle, the pressure in your tires should be correct. If the pressure is too high or too low, the tire won't behave properly. Too much air pressure may cause the tire to wear improperly or to explode. Too little pressure will cause the tires to wear quickly and waste energy. By maintaining the correct tire pressure, you won't have to buy tires as often and will use less energy getting from place to place.

The energy needed to roll a tire a given distance increases when you have less pressure in the tires because friction is greater. Rolling friction opposes the tire's motion, and with a larger force opposing it, more energy is needed to keep it moving. (Energy equals work, which is force times distance.) Rolling friction occurs because the tire changes shape as it rolls. In order to change shape, forces must be exerted by the road on the tire through a distance. That means work is done. Some of this work is returned to the car because the tire acts as a rubber band and springs back into place, but some energy is lost to heat as parts of the tire rub on other parts or the road. With more pressure, the tire changes its shape less so less energy is needed.

You can run experiments in a number of ways to find how rolling friction changes with differences in air pressure. However, an easy way uses a bicycle with training wheels.

The training wheels allow you to pull the bike slowly without having it fall over. By changing the air pressure in the tires, you can see how the frictional forces change.

MATERIALS AND TOOLS

flat area to ride a bicycle safely
rope
bicycle with training wheels
spring scale
friend (small enough to ride the bicycle)
pressure gauge
air pump to pump up the tires

NOTE: Don't put more air pressure in the tire than the manufacturer recommends. The maximum is printed on the tire. Overinflating a tire can cause it to burst, and this can be dangerous. You will also have to replace the tire.

Find a flat, safe area for riding the bike. A sidewalk may be a good place unless too many people are using it. Tie the rope to the handlebars of a bicycle with training wheels and attach the spring scale to the rope as in Figure 2. Now, walk at a constant speed and find the force needed to pull the bicycle. Find the pressure in the tires with the pressure gauge and record both values. Remember, even a slight hill can make a difference in the force required to pull the bicycle. To avoid any errors associated with hills, always make your measurements as you pull the bike in the same direction on the same section of pavement. If you pull the bike in a different direction, you will introduce another variable into the experiment. You will not have a "controlled" experiment.

Now, let a little air out of the tires and find the new pressure in the tires. Find how much force is needed to pull the bicycle at the same constant speed as before. Record the force and pressure.

Keep letting air out of the tires until the tires are so flat

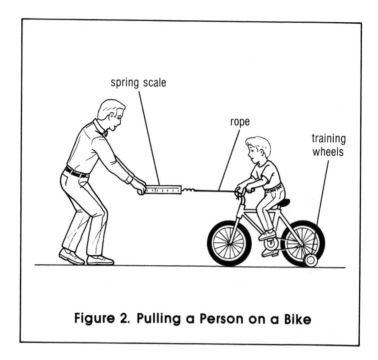

spring scale

rope

training
wheels

Figure 2. Pulling a Person on a Bike

that the metal rims almost bump the ground. If the place where you are riding is bumpy, be careful not to dent the rims. That can happen if you hit a bump when the pressure is low. When you are finished taking data, pump air back into the tires. Make sure to inflate the tires to the recommended pressure.

What changes do you notice in the amount of force required to pull your friend on the bicycle? If the amount of work you do equals the product of force times distance, how does the amount of work change as the pressure changes?

OTHER PROJECTS
WITH ROLLING FRICTION

1. Try running the experiment with a person of a different weight on the bicycle. Record the weight of the person and the force needed to pull the bicycle with different tire pressures. A large change in weight will cause larger differences in the force, so find a person who weighs quite a bit more or less than the first person. On the basis of your data, do you think car manufacturers would make their cars heavier or lighter to reduce rolling friction?

2. Run your experiment using tires with different treads. Mountain bike treads tend to be "knobby" and are very different from racing bike treads. What are the differences in rolling friction?

3. Try your experiment on different surfaces. Mountain bike riders ride on sand, smooth trails, rocky trails and mud. Can you predict what changes in rolling friction will occur when the bike is pulled on different surfaces? Compare the force for different types of tires on different surfaces.

4. Design a system in which the rolling friction is the lowest possible and run an experiment to test whether your ideas are correct.

5. Try rolling different kinds of balls on different surfaces and see how rolling friction changes. Do the distances the balls roll before stopping seem reasonable?

STRING TRIMMERS

String trimmers are neat little machines. They spin a plastic string around in circles to cut down weeds and long grass. Because the "cutting" is done by plastic, if you hit a rock or hard object with the string, you don't get sparks or pieces of rock and metal flying through the air. Also, instead of having to sharpen the blade or replace it you just pull out some more string. *Remember.* When you use any string trimmer, you need protective eyewear and clothing be-cause small bits of weeds or other objects can hurt your eyes or skin.

How are the weeds cut and what would make an ideal

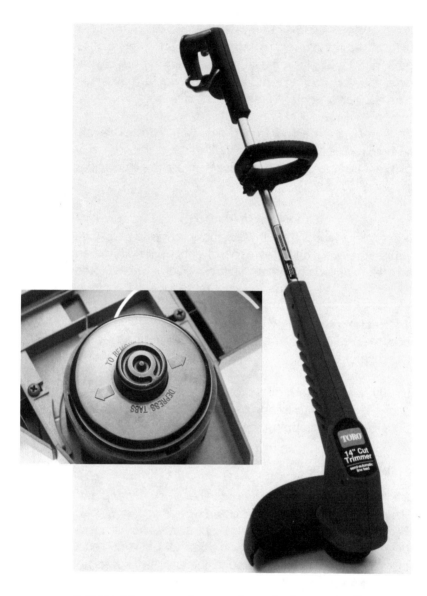

A string trimmer cuts grass by spinning a plastic string rapidly in circles along the ground. The inset shows the underside of the string trimmer, where the white string can be seen coming from the motor.

string trimmer? Energy from either electricity or gasoline makes the string move in circles and cut weeds. But is it possible to make one that works on person power? Can you figure how long the string on a trimmer should be to be most efficient? If you use a real string trimmer, make sure an adult knows what experiments you will be doing.

A string trimmer is just a string going in circles. Sir Isaac Newton's laws help explain how the trimmers work. One of his laws states that an object in motion tends to stay in motion and an object at rest tends to stay at rest. The moving string wants to stay moving and the weed, which is stationary, wants to stay at rest. When the string hits the weed, a force changes the motion of the string: it slows it down. A force is also exerted on a small area of the weed. This force may make that small section move while the rest of the weed resists motion. If the small section moves, the weed is cut!

But what makes an efficient weed trimmer? Generally, the faster the string goes, the more force it exerts on the weed. The string's speed is determined by the spin rate of the trimmer and the length of the string, which is the radius of the circle the string makes. The tip of the string travels one circumference (2π x [radius]) each spin. With a longer radius, it goes farther and therefore faster if the trimmer spins at a constant rate.

You can do a simple experiment to investigate how a string trimmer operates. Other experiments can be more complex, but you should start with an easy one.

MATERIALS AND TOOLS

    meter stick
    rope such as clothesline
    stopwatch
    paper
    tape
    weight

With the stick, measure a one-meter (3-ft) long section of rope. In an area where you will not hit anything or anyone, swing the rope in a circle as fast as you can. (Outdoors may be the best place for the experiment.) Use a stopwatch to find the time it takes for one swing.

Now, tape a piece of paper to a support and tape a weight to the bottom of the paper as shown in Figure 3.

Then, swing the rope around in a circle as before and see whether you can cut the paper with it. Record the results.

Repeat the experiment by swinging the rope around in circles at the same rate as before but using rope 0.5 m (1.5 ft) long. Record your results.

Figure 3. Being a String Trimmer

Repeat your experiment with longer and shorter ropes. Make sure to spin the rope at the same rate in each test. Record the length of rope, what happens to the paper, and any other observations you have. Was it easy or hard to spin at the constant rate? What happened to the cutting ability of the rope? And so on.

What conclusions can you draw about how the length of the rope affects the ability to cut the paper? Is there a "best" length? Why is it the best? What length uses energy most efficiently?

OTHER PROJECTS
WITH STRING TRIMMERS

1.   Try running your experiment with different spin rates. See what results you get.

2.   Try different types of rope. Use thicker or thinner ropes of different materials. What results do you observe?

3.   Get a string trimmer and see whether your observations with models of string trimmers agree with the operation of a real one. Run these experiments *only* with the permission of an adult and use safety precautions. Always wear protective eyewear, long pants, and thick shoes or boots and be careful of those around you.

4.   Use a string trimmer and run tests to see what kinds of weeds can be cut down. Does the trimmer work better on dead or live weeds? Can you find the parts of the broken weeds and see how the weed broke? How do different sizes of weed trimmer string stand up to the task of cutting weeds before they break? How do they compare in their ability to cut weeds?

GEARS, BICYCLES,
AND OTHER THINGS

Bicycles use gears to make pedaling more efficient. Gears are used in cars, clocks, machines, and almost everything with moving parts. Gears allow one part of a machine to turn at one speed and another part to turn at another. They can make things move faster or exert larger forces. Gears allow for a more efficient use of energy.

Gears on a bicycle allow you to go faster than you can go on a tricycle, which has no gears. On mountain bikes, the gears also allow you to go up steeper hills than you can on regular bikes. But how do gears really help? Why do some gear combinations do particular things?

The work you do on the pedals is changed to work to make the bicycle move. Work is the product of force times distance ($W = fd$). You move the pedals down a distance as you exert a force. This causes the wheel to turn a certain distance and exert a force. You can run experiments to see how different combinations of gears get you up different hills. What combinations do you think will be best and which ones worst?

MATERIALS AND TOOLS

    scale
    bicycle
    meter stick
    protractor

Use the scale to find your weight. Record this value.

As you pedal, the pedals move in a circle. Find the diameter of that circle with the meter stick and record it.

Now, record the combinations of gears that you can get with your bicycle. Then, for each combination measure the distance the bicycle moves when a pedal goes from

**The gears on a bicycle make it
easier to go fast and to climb hills.**

its highest position to its lowest position, as shown in Figure 4.

Use the following equation to find the average force exerted by the wheels in each of the different gears.

$$\text{FORCE} = \frac{(\text{your weight}) \times (\text{diameter of pedal circle})}{(\text{distance moved by bicycle})}$$

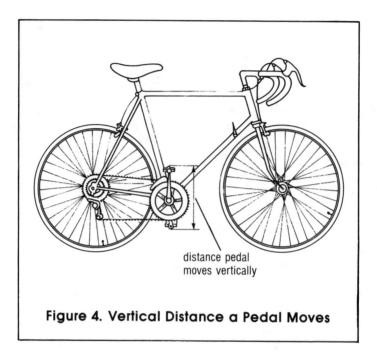

distance pedal
moves vertically

Figure 4. Vertical Distance a Pedal Moves

With this information, find a hill that changes its steep-ness. Make sure that you are going to be safe as you ride your bike on this hill and are not going to be injured in any way. Use your protractor to find the angle of the slope, or how steep a particular section of the hill is. Then, find the gear that allows you to get up the hill at a constant speed. Stand on the pedals but don't pull up on the handlebars, because that will add to the force you exert. For this experi-ment, you are trying to use a constant force, which is your weight. Remember to maintain a constant speed. If you are increasing your speed, use a higher gear; if you are slowing down, use a lower gear.

When you have found the gear for one steepness of hill, try other places on the hill with different angles. Record your data. Do the results agree with what you would expect from the amount of force the wheels exert?

OTHER PROJECTS WITH GEARS

1. Put a scale against a pedal of a bike and see how much force you can exert when you stand on the pedal and pull on the handlebars. See whether the increased force increases the steepness of hill you can climb. Does the result agree with what you expect?

2. Take apart an unrepairable tape deck, camera, or other machine with moving parts. *Do not* plug in the device after you have taken it apart because you may harm yourself or start a fire. See whether you can figure out how the motor and gears make the machine work. (In some devices, pulleys act as gears when belts go around large and small pulleys.) A tape deck needs to make the tape move past the heads and then the tape must be wound on the take-up reel. Do different wheels turn at different speeds? Do the gears behave like those on a bicycle? How are they different?

3. Find a motor and then design a set of gears that will allow your motor to run a clock that keeps good time. If you can find appropriate gears (American Science & Surplus, 7605 Howard Street, Skokie, IL 60076, is a good source), build the clock and see whether it works.

4. Compare car specifications given by manufacturers (found at car dealers) to see how the engine rotation rate changes in different gears for different cars. Car engines do not perform efficiently when they turn too slowly or too quickly. Can you find the number of revolutions per minute (RPM) the engine makes when it is operating the most efficiently?

ENERGY IN RUBBER BANDS AND SPRINGS

Rubber bands and springs are used to power many toys. You put energy into the rubber band by twisting it or stretching it, or you put energy into a spring by stretching it or compressing it. But how much energy do you put into the rubber band or spring? Is it predictable or random?

You can run experiments to investigate how energy is stored in rubber bands. First, you might want to develop a hypothesis or a guess as to the answer. Then you can test your guess and find out whether you are right. Ask yourself some questions and then get started.

MATERIALS AND TOOLS

    block of wood
    small nail and hammer
    rubber bands
    meter stick

Take a small block of wood and nail a small nail into the smallest side of the block. Then use the hammer to bend the nail into a hook shape. Then attach a few rubber bands (tied together) to the hook.

Place the block on a table or on a floor with no rugs. Pull the rubber bands so they are straight but not exerting any force. Now, while holding the rubber band in one place, move the block to stretch the rubber band, as shown in Figure 5. By trial and error, find the distance that you must stretch the rubber band so that the block returns to its original position when released. With a meter stick, measure this distance as precisely as possible and record it.

Now, stretch the rubber band twice as far as before and release it. Measure the distance you stretch the rubber band and the total distance the block slides as precisely as possible. Record these values. Repeat the experiment a

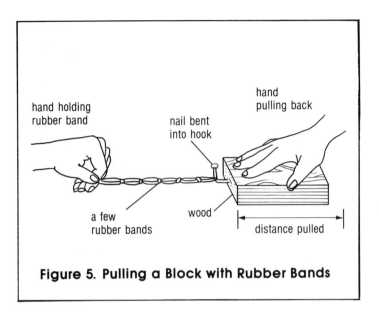

Figure 5. Pulling a Block with Rubber Bands

couple of times to check your results. Make sure that the block slides rather than flies through the air and that the surface it slides on is uniform.

Repeat your experiment with different amounts of stretching.

The amount of energy you put into your rubber band is directly related to the distance the block slides. It should slide twice as far with twice as much energy. How does the amount of energy change as you change the amount of stretch? Is this the result expected? Can you make a graph of stretch versus energy to show your results more clearly?

OTHER PROJECTS WITH RUBBER BANDS AND SPRINGS

1. Repeat your experiments with different combinations of rubber bands. What happens if the rubber bands are shorter or longer, thicker or thinner?

2. What happens if you use springs? Use stretchy springs that you can pull quite easily but be careful not to pull them too far. When springs are stretched too far, they never return to their original length.

3. Draw graphs of energy stored compared to the amount of stretching for a number of different combinations of springs and rubber bands. How are the graphs similar? How are they different? Can you explain why your graphs look the way they do?

4. Use a spring that can be compressed or stretched and see whether as much energy is stored when the spring is compressed a given distance as when it is stretched the same distance.

5. Design and build a launcher so that you can send an object through the air a predictable distance by stretching a rubber band or spring a given distance. Be careful not to injure yourself or anyone else with your flying object.

6. Design and run an experiment to see how the twisting of rubber bands stores energy. Does twice the twisting produce twice the energy? Is energy stored in a way similar to stretching the rubber band? Are there differences? What happens when knots start to form in the rubber band?

7. Design and build a rubber band-powered car or airplane. See how the amount of twisting or stretching changes the distance traveled.

SPINNING BASKETBALLS: ENGINEERING A PERFECT SHOT

Basketball is a sport that uses a number of scientific principles. Players launch a projectile at a hoop and hope that it goes in. The projectile follows the laws of physics just as

**A bow and arrow is a good example of how
energy can be stored in a string by stretching it.
By pulling back the bowstring, this girl is
storing energy that will launch the arrow.**

rocks or other objects do. But players also use spin to help them score points. A properly spinning basketball has a greater chance of going into the hoop than one that is not spinning. But which way should it spin and how much does it affect the shot?

If the basketball goes right through the hoop, obviously

spin does not matter. Spin helps only when the ball hits something before it goes through. When the ball arrives at the basket, it has energy of motion. This energy may cause the ball to bounce away from the rim rather than through it. The spin can take away some energy and make the ball stay closer to the hoop.

A spinning ball has what is called rotational energy. This energy can change the motion of a ball after it bounces. Rotational energy exists in all rotating objects. If you accidentally put your fingers into the spokes of a spinning bicycle wheel, the energy will do work (exert a force for a distance) on your fingers. Ouch!

Running experiments with a spinning ball isn't terribly easy because it is hard to get precise numbers. However, you may see your shot improve, and you may win more games after doing a little research. If you don't play basketball, you may be able to show someone else why and how he or she should spin the ball.

MATERIALS AND TOOLS

    basketball
    meter stick
    tape
    basketball hoop

Start by running a few simple experiments, and then try to apply what you learn to shooting baskets.

First, drop the ball and see how it bounces. Then, from the same height, drop the ball but make it spin before it leaves your hands. Observe what happens to the ball, and record your observations. Now, change the amount of spin and see whether the results are predictable.

Now, choose a spot on the floor to throw the ball from and with a meter stick measure a distance of 2 meters from that spot. Mark this spot with a little bit of tape. Next, throw the ball gently through the air so that it lands on that spot.

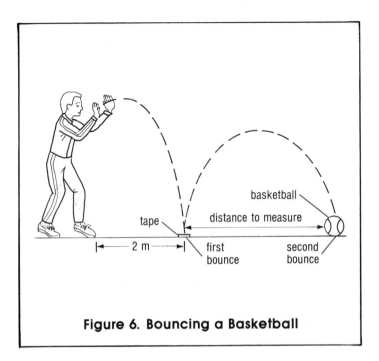

Figure 6. Bouncing a Basketball

Measure the distance between the first and second bounce as in Figure 6. Throw it with no spin initially and then throw it with spin. Change the spin so that it is forward spin and then back spin. Record your data. What differences do you observe? Can you get the ball to stop moving horizontally and just bounce up and down? Why might this be an advantage when you are shooting a basketball?

Finally, shoot baskets from a place where you normally can get the ball into the hoop quite frequently. Shoot the ball with different amounts of spin: back spin, forward spin, and no spin. Record what happens to the ball. Can you make any general statements about how the ball behaves near the basket with a particular spin? (If it goes through the hoop without touching anything, spin does not matter. I wish I could do that all the time!)

What conclusions can you draw from your experiments? What happens when the ball hits the front of the hoop or the back? What happens if it hits the backboard first? When is it a disadvantage to have spin?

OTHER PROJECTS
WITH SPINNING BALLS

1. Hoola Hoops are large plastic rings about (1 m) 3 ft in diameter. If you make them spin when you throw them away from you along the floor, you can make them return to you. Is there a minimum amount of spin needed to do this? Does the surface they land on make a difference?

2. Run experiments with rubber balls or "superballs" to see how spin affects their motion. What is required to stop the forward progress of the ball? Will it remain stationary after the first bounce? If so, why?

3. When a yo-yo spins down to the ground and you let go of the string just as it reaches the ground, it starts rolling off. Why does it do this? Is the rate that it rolls along the ground related to the rate which it is spinning before it hits the ground?

4. If you have access to a video camera and a video player that can play individual frames (so you can see one picture, analyze it, push a button and see the next picture taken an instant later), you can analyze the motion of a basketball more precisely. Take videos of basketballs thrown with forward spin, backward spin, and no spin. You will need a dozen or more shots with each type of spin. Play individual frames and observe the rotation rate, and then plot the motion of the ball around the hoop. Remember, the closer the ball is to the hoop after it hits the first time, the more chance it has to go into the hoop after the bounce.

5. If you have access to the type of video camera discussed in number 4, try analyzing the motion of a spinning rubber ball as it bounces. You may have to put a mark on the ball so that you can see its spin rate. Look at the velocity of impact, the spin rate, and the angle at which the ball bounces. What affects the way the ball bounces? Does changing the spin rate change the angle of bounce by a predictable amount? Can you build a machine that puts a certain spin on the ball so that you can get the ball to bounce the same way each time it leaves the machine? How does the surface the ball bounces on change the way it bounces? (When tennis is played on different surfaces such as clay, pavement, and grass, the game changes a bit for this reason.)

TORQUE CONVERTERS
AND AUTOMATIC SHIFTS

Torque converters may sound like strange things but they are in all automatic-shift cars. They make propellers turn in airplanes, and they show up in many other places. A torque converter transfers the rotational energy of one rotating object to another. Often the system allows the motor to turn at one speed and the wheels to turn at a number of different speeds as in a car.

Basically, the system is two objects that can rotate. They are separated by a small distance with a fluid in between. If one object starts turning, frictional forces exerted by the fluid cause the other object to rotate. The fluid acts to connect the two objects.

The torque converter (automatic shift) in a car allows the motor to turn while the wheels are stopped because there is no direct connection. When you want to start the car moving, you take your foot off the brake and frictional forces in the fluid make the car move.

You can build a model of a torque converter using two

disks. But how are the disks constructed? Should they have rough surfaces or smooth? How close should they be to each other? How should the fluid behave?

MATERIALS AND TOOLS

jigsaw
thin plywood (¼ in or 6 mm)
wooden spool
nails
drill bits
large lead fishing sinkers
hammer
permanent marker
tuna fish can
waterproof glue
weights (sand or rocks)
clamp
battery-operated drill
extension bit for drill
circular sanding pad for drill
bucket large enough to hold apparatus
timer
tape

NOTE: A battery-operated drill is the only kind you should use for this experiment. Other electric drills can cause dangerous shocks because the drill will be used near water.

With a jigsaw and the help of an adult, cut a disk 20 cm (8 in) in diameter from plywood. Find a wooden spool and then get a nail that is slightly longer than the length of the spool plus the thickness of the plywood as shown in Figure 7. Ideally, the nail would be 6 mm (¼ in) longer than this length. The nail will be the axle. Find the center of the disk and drill a hole slightly smaller in diameter than the nail.

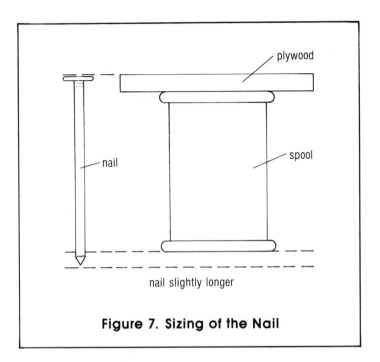

plywood

nail

spool

nail slightly longer

Figure 7. Sizing of the Nail

The disk must be weighted so that it sinks in water. Weight the disk by using large lead fishing weights nailed to the bottom of the disk. The weights should be added in pairs with each pair opposite each other as shown in Figure 8. Any nails poking through onto the top should be hammered over so they are not dangerous. Now, make a short dark line with a permanent marker in one spot at the edge of the disk.

Find a tuna fish can or other can that is much wider than it is high. Remove the top and carefully put tape over the sharp edges. Use waterproof glue according to the manufacturer's directions to glue the spool to the center of the can and the nail in the hole through the plywood disk. After the glue has dried, put the axle into the spool as in Figure 9 and test to see that the disk spins easily. Now,

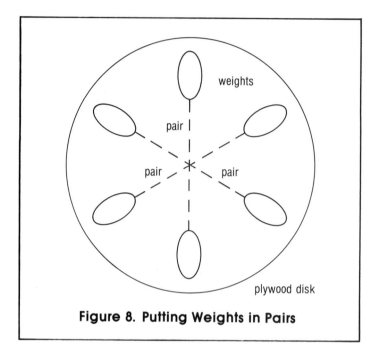

Figure 8. Putting Weights in Pairs

remove the axle and weight the can with rocks or sand and tape the weight in. The can should sink in water.

Now, find a clamp that can hold a battery-operated drill. The clamp must hold the drill at precise positions. The extension bit is needed to keep the drill away from water. Finally, you need a sanding pad that is attached to the extension bit of a drill. Your apparatus should look like that in Figure 9.

It is now time to start experimenting. Place the tuna can and disk in a bucket and add water to cover the disk by about 6 cm (2 in). Adjust the drill in the clamp so the sanding disk is about 1 cm (⅓ in) away from the wooden disk. Turn on the drill, and the wooden disk should start to spin, too. Time how long it takes for the wooden disk to turn once by observing the black mark move. If nothing happens,

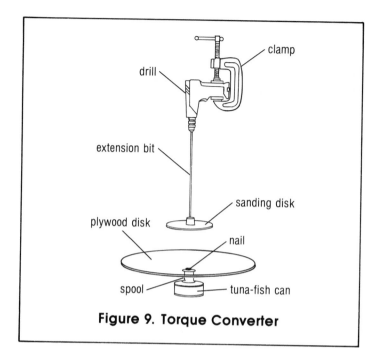

Figure 9. Torque Converter

something may be sticking or you may have to add "roughness" to the sanding disk by attaching tape to it (as described later). If the disk rises up and hits the sanding disk, add more lead weights to the disk.

Now, vary the distance between the disks and see how the time for one revolution changes. The faster the disk turns, the more rotational energy is being transferred with your torque converter. Use a constant speed for your drill for all experiments. Record the separation distance and the time it takes to turn one revolution for each trial.

Now, dry off the sanding disk and add tape in ridges to make a rougher surface. Make a ridge of tape by folding the tape over in the center as shown in Figure 10. Vary the distance between the disks as before and measure the force. Are the results what you would expect?

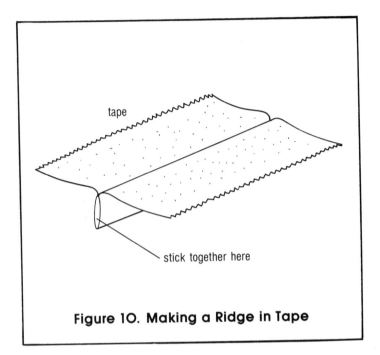

tape

stick together here

Figure 1O. Making a Ridge in Tape

OTHER PROJECTS
WITH TORQUE CONVERTERS

1. Vary the "roughness" of the plywood disk by adding tape to it and see the results. (You will probably have to let the wood dry for the tape to stick.) You might also stick small pieces of wood to the disk using rubber cement to produce the same effect. Does the positioning of the pieces of wood or tape make a difference?

2. Find out whether the drill's rotation speed makes a difference in the amount of frictional force produced.

3. The fluid you use makes a difference. A less viscous fluid flows more easily and causes less friction. Try adding dishwashing liquid to the water to reduce the viscosity. Do not use any dangerous fluids; check with an adult before using fluids other than water or soapy water.

4. Find a car mechanic who will show you how a real automatic shift system works. If you can see the inside of one, then you can understand what is happening. How is your torque converter similar and how is it different from the one in an automatic shift?

DESIGNING A ROCKING CHAIR

A rocking chair is a delightful thing. The rocking may put a crying baby to sleep or it may just soothe the soul. You put in a little energy and the chair moves back and forth. A scientist would say you give the chair kinetic energy, or energy of motion, which is then changed into potential energy, or energy of position. The rocking changes kinetic into potential and back to kinetic in a soothing way.

But what factors affect the way a rocking chair rocks? Can the rockers be of any shape or must they be of a particular shape to make a good rocking chair? So what are the important characteristics of a good rocking chair? It shouldn't tip over and you shouldn't have to work very hard to rock it. How can you design a good one?

Think about what shape the rockers must be and how they should be placed on the chair. Develop a hypothesis and then test it by experiment. Are your instincts correct?

MATERIALS AND TOOLS

old chair
½ in (1.3 cm)-thick plywood
jigsaw
C-clamps
pencil
paper

The rockers on the chair to the left have a greater curve than those on the chair to the right. The difference in design means the chair to the right has a gentler rocking motion.

Get permission to use an old chair that may be scratched during this project. With the help of an adult cut two pieces of plywood 30 cm by 90 cm (12 in by 36 in). These will be the "rockers."

With the C-clamps, attach one piece to one side of the chair and one to the other as shown in Figure 11 so that the plywood lifts the chair about 5 cm (2 in) off the floor. Have equal amounts of plywood sticking out in front of the chair as the back. Mark the position of the C-clamps on the plywood with the pencil.

Now, draw a curve on the plywood in the shape of a rocker, as in Figure 11, and then remove the plywood from the chair. With the help of an adult, cut along the curve with the jigsaw. Start by cutting off only a small amount

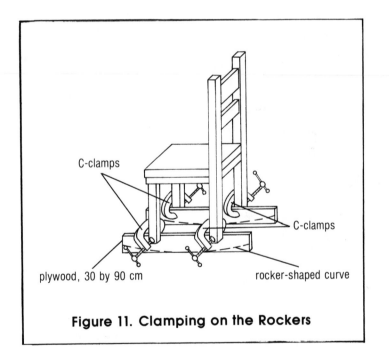

C-clamps

C-clamps

plywood, 30 by 90 cm

rocker-shaped curve

Figure 11. Clamping on the Rockers

of wood, because you will cut more and more as your experiment continues. Make both rockers the same shape.

Then, reattach the rockers and record observations about how well it rocks. Is it easy or hard? Does the chair seem unstable or stable? Trace the shape of the rocker on a large piece of paper and label your observations and the shape as "Trial #1."

Now, draw a slightly different curve on the rockers and cut off a little more wood. A small change in shape can make a large difference. Be careful not to injure yourself with the saw. Repeat your observations.

Keep modifying the curve of the rockers and record your observations. If your chair becomes too unstable, you can use another pair of 30 cm by 90 cm plywood pieces placed higher up the legs so that it acts as a stop, as in Figure 12.

OTHER PROJECTS WITH FURNITURE

1. After you have experimented with your first plywood rockers, see whether you can design better ones that are all one piece and don't need a second piece of plywood to make the chair stable. Does the curve on the front have to be different from the curve on the back to make it rock comfortably?

2. Can you make a rocking chair that is so unstable you don't want to sit in it but that looks like a normal rocking chair? *Caution:* This chair might injure some unsuspecting person so you should not leave these rockers on the chair when you are not around.

3. Build an apparatus for designing a chair to fit you perfectly. Say you want a chair to use in front of a computer. Design a system so that you can adjust the height of the front of the seat, the back of the seat, the angle of the seat,

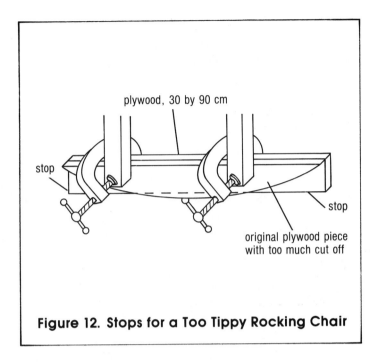

plywood, 30 by 90 cm

stop

stop

original plywood piece
with too much cut off

Figure 12. Stops for a Too Tippy Rocking Chair

and the back support. You should also be able to adjust the armrest height. When you have the perfect chair, build one out of plywood and see whether it feels as good as you expect. Remember, everyone has a different shape so everyone has a different "perfect" chair. Because you sit in a different way when you eat at a dinner table, design a chair for that purpose. You might use this apparatus to build custom-designed chairs.

OTHER PROJECTS WITH ENERGY

1. Investigate how streamlining helps make a bicycle go faster down a hill. You have potential energy at the top of the hill, and you go faster if you lose less of that energy to friction from air moving across your body. What differences occur when you sit differently on the bike? What streamlining can you add to the bike to make it go faster? Be careful in all your experiments not to injure yourself or others.

2. Design a car that uses a mousetrap as an energy source. With a limited amount of energy, how must you design your car to make it go a long distance?

3. Design a raft with paddle wheels that you turn with pedals. Then, experiment with the size, shape, and number of paddles on the wheel to make the most efficient use of your paddling energy.

4. Think about some of the devices you have around the house such as a jar opener. Can you design one that is safe and efficient and is different from any that you have seen? Be careful in your experiments not to injure yourself.

5. Build a model sailboat, and experiment with different sails to find which uses the energy of the wind most efficiently.

6. Engineer a system so that with a small amount of energy, you can open or close the door to your room from your bed.

7. Build a drawing machine like the one in Figure 13 that can enlarge or reduce the size of drawings. How can you make the machine so that it doesn't wobble and draws a good copy of the original?

8. Build a solar-powered car or boat. You may want to use photoelectric cells, but other methods exist.

9. Build a wind tunnel so that you can find what shapes are the most efficient moving through the air. The more

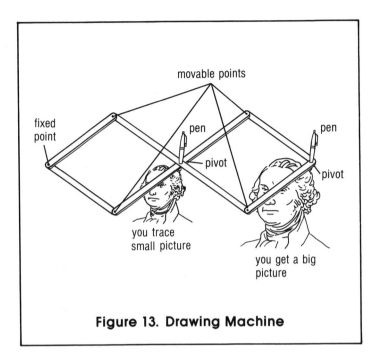

Figure 13. Drawing Machine

easily a car moves through the air, for instance, the less gasoline it uses per mile.

10. Design and build models of bridges and see which ones are the strongest. Of course, using more materials makes them stronger, but you might see how light you can make a bridge that holds a given weight.

4

ENGINEERING AND
THE ENVIRONMENT

Some engineers try to save the environment. They design things that save energy, reduce pollution, or do both. Some engineers work at building better windmills or solar collectors because they produce forms of energy that are pollution free. However, solar systems must collect the energy efficiently before they are practical. Other engineers work on detecting pollution sources. For instance, about 1 percent of the cars on the road produce 50 percent of the pollution. If these cars could be identified as they drove down the road, only they would need to be checked and repaired. Engineers also work on building energy-efficient structures. Because large amounts of energy are used for heating and cooling, better insulation or more efficient furnaces and air conditioners could help.

Many problems face engineers working to save the environment. Sometimes a solution creates other problems or costs too much money. If making more efficient insulation for a house causes pollution or uses hazardous materials, it may never be used. If the solar hot water heater freezes in the winter and breaks the pipes, it is not useful. Engineers must be realistic about costs, both in dollars and to the environment, and they must also think about how people will use the things they design.

If you are interested in helping to clean up the environment, save energy, or reduce pollution, you can run experiments and design systems to try to solve problems. Your experiments may start out quite simple but may become more complex. Your experiments may give you some ideas that no one else had thought of. By asking questions and then running experiments to find answers, you may discover something. You may also become interested in doing more experiments and eventually become an engineer. People are not born with a label that says, "Make me an engineer." People develop an interest and then follow their own paths to engineering. You may find that engineering becomes your life's work, and you might help our planet. At the very least, you will learn something about science and then can better understand what scientists can and cannot do to save the environment.

WINDMILLS

Windmills are used to generate electricity or pump water. They consist of two or more blades and a drive system. Wind mills in Holland typically have four blades; those used for pumping water in the American West have a few dozen; and more modern ones have two or three. Obviously, engineers have built windmills in different ways over the years. They have also used different materials. But what makes a good windmill? What is the best number of blades to use, and how should they be attached to the drive system?

A windmill uses the wind to exert forces on the blades, which move; therefore, work is done by the wind (work = force x distance). One of Sir Isaac Newton's laws states that an object in motion tends to stay in motion unless acted on by a force. As air moves past the windmill, the air changes

These modern windmills generate electricity on a wind energy farm in the Tehachapi Mountains in California.

direction, so the windmill must exert a force on the air. Newton also said that for every force there is an equal and opposite force. Therefore, if the windmill exerts a force on the air, the air exerts a force on the windmill. But how can the force be made as large as possible? What are the characteristics of an efficient windmill? Make a hypothesis and then test your ideas.

MATERIALS AND TOOLS

Tinker-Toy set that includes two free-spinning axles
cardboard
string
cup
weights, large and small
fan
protractor
balance

Build a windmill out of Tinker-Toys or similar materials with four cardboard blades as in Figure 14. The main axis should be supported by two free-spinning axles and should extend about 7.5 cm (3 in) beyond the axles on the end opposite the blades. The blades should be on short wooden sticks and measure about 2.5 by 10 cm (1 in by 4 in) as shown.

Set the windmill on a table with the end opposite the blades hanging off the table. Tie a string to the axle tightly so it won't slip, and tie the other end to a small paper or plastic cup. Add some large weights to hold the windmill in place. Now, place a fan on the table about 1 m (3 ft) away.

Using a protractor, adjust the windmill blades so that each blade is at a 45° angle to the direction from which the fan will blow. Now, turn on the fan to the lowest speed and see how much weight you need to add to the cup to prevent the windmill from turning. You will probably have to hold the windmill blades and then add weight until the weights prevent rotation. If the windmill doesn't move when there are no weights in the cup, then use a higher fan speed, move the fan closer to the windmill, or use a lighter cup. Turn off the fan and find the mass of the cup and the weights with a balance. Record the mass, the angle of the blades, the speed setting on the fan, and the distance from the fan to the windmill.

Next, change the angle of the blades to 30°. Turn on the fan, find the weight that will stop the blades, and record

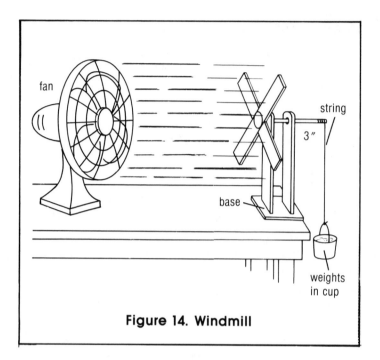

fan

string

3″

base

weights
in cup

Figure 14. Windmill

the data. Repeat your experiment with other angles between 0° and 90°. Record all the appropriate data.

Which angle seems to produce the most force?

OTHER PROJECTS WITH WINDMILLS

1. Using the apparatus described, change the number of blades on the windmill. Try two, six, and eight. Does double the number of blades cause double the force with a given wind speed? Does the best angle change?

2. Change the wind speed and see whether the angle for most force is still the same. Try to measure the speed of the wind and see how much more force occurs with twice the wind speed. A crude way to measure the wind speed is to let a piece of paper move in the wind and measure how long it takes to go a distance. The speed is hard to measure because the paper moves quickly. Your science teacher may have equipment that can get better results, such as a photogate (a timer that starts and stops when an object breaks a light beam).

3. Change the size of the blades on your windmill. Does doubling the size double the force?

4. Try making blades that are not just flat pieces of cardboard. Make one side flat and the other side curved like an airplane wing. Adjust the angle of these blades and see what happens to the force. Does a curved blade give more or less force than a flat blade of similar size? Is the angle for most force the same?

5. Having stationary blades is not realistic because windmills must turn to do work. The turning blades make the wind behave differently as it goes past them. Run experiments where the windmill winds up the string at a constant rate. Adjust the weight in the cup so that the cup is raised a certain distance in a certain amount of time. Change the angle of the blades and see what angle lifts the most weight. Do you get the same angle with the blades that are shaped like airplane wings?

6. Try building blades that are "twisted," meaning that the angle near the axle is different from the angle near the tip. Airplane propellers are shaped this way. Is there a difference in the way the windmill behaves?

WAVE ENERGY

Waves crash on beaches and release huge amounts of energy. Storms have enough energy to move sandbars, destroy houses, and cause great amounts of damage. This energy source can be tapped to generate electricity, but it is not easy. The problem is that waves are sometimes small and sometimes large. The small waves have little energy and the large ones can destroy the device collecting the energy.

The energy in waves is related to the square of their height. If the height is doubled, the energy is four times as great. If the height is tripled, the energy is nine times as great ($2^2 = 4$ and $3^3 = 9$). But how can this energy be harnessed? What devices can turn wave energy into useful energy?

Engineers are working on a number of possible ways to collect the energy, but a leading method being tried relies on air. When the waves come in, they push water into a container and push air out. The air moves past a windmill or turbine and generates electricity. But what factors affect how much energy is generated? How can a system be designed to give the most energy output? What design problems does an engineer encounter when designing such a system?

MATERIALS AND TOOLS

plywood
jigsaw
waterproof glue
meter stick
permanent marker
10 cm (4-in)-diameter flexible plastic pipe 1 m (3 ft)
   long
small DC fan
ammeter
garbage can filled with water
watch

Build a box 0.5 m by 0.5 m by 1 m deep (1.5 ft by 1.5 ft by 3 ft deep) out of plywood using waterproof glue. The bot-

In this wave energy system developed
at Edinburgh University in Scotland, the
bobbing of the individual sections on the waves
drives rotary pumps in the spine of the system.
The spine is about a mile long, and the pumps can
generate as much as 50 megawatts of electricity.

tom of the box should be open. Cut a hole in the top of
the box so that you can insert the plastic pipe into the box.
*Get an adult to help cut the wood because any saw can
be dangerous.*

Use the meter stick to make a scale with a permanent
marker on the side of the box to show how far you move
the box into the water. Connect the fan to the plastic pipe

with waterproof glue or tape so that any air going through the pipe will go through the fan. Connect the wires from the fan to a DC ammeter (this can be a multimeter). Next, use waterproof glue or tape to attach the pipe to the hole in the top of the box with the fan at the top, as in Figure 15.

Now, fill the garbage can with water and put the box into the water. Air should escape from the box through the pipe and make the fan turn. Make sure that the ammeter and fan are in a place where they will not get wet. This is why a long section of plastic pipe is used.

Now, move the box down into the water and observe the current generated by the fan. The fan is acting as a windmill. If you observe a current, then start to gather data. If you don't observe a current, you may need a more sensitive ammeter.

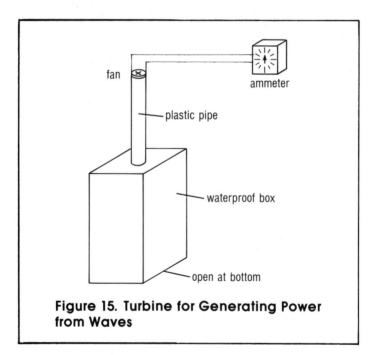

Figure 15. Turbine for Generating Power from Waves

Now, starting with the bottom of the box just in the water, quickly move the box down 15 cm (6 in). Observe the current, and with a watch, time how long it takes before the current stops. Record this information.

Repeat your measurements when you move the box down 30 cm (12 in), 45 cm (18 in), and so on. Does the amount of current and the amount of time for the current to stop change as you would expect? Moving the box downward simulates waves. Instead of the water level moving up around the box, you are moving the box up and down.

Move the box downward half as fast and see the results. What happens with the current and time? Are the results what you would expect?

Electric power is related to the current squared. Twice the current means four times the power. How does the power generated relate to the amount that you move the box?

OTHER PROJECTS
WITH WAVE GENERATORS

1. Design a system that will let you move the box down and back up, with the air moving in only one direction— out the pipe past the fan. You will have to build a flap system where the air can go in a hole but not go out past the flap. The flap (perhaps made out of rubber or plastic) acts as a one-way valve. Using this valve, see how the current changes as you move the box in and out of the water.

2. Design a system using flexible pipes and one-way valves in which air flows past the fan in the same direction regardless of whether the box is moving down or up. You will have to make a few one-way valves and perhaps build a box for the fan to sit in. By generating power when you move the box down or up, you get twice the power.

3. Take your system to a body of water with waves and see whether the results you get in the garbage can are similar to the results you get with real waves. Make sure that you protect your meter and fan from water damage.

4. Try designing a system that makes wheels turn without using air moving past a fan or turbine. You can design something similar to a car engine where a piston moves in and out and causes the drive shaft to turn. See if you can design a system like this that generates more power than an air system.

A PASSIVE SOLAR-HEATED HOUSE

Passive solar heating is an economical way to use solar energy. Solar energy is collected by windows that are a part of the building. In the United States, south facing windows in a house collect solar energy while north facing ones never collect any. When building a house, put more windows on the south side to save energy.

A greenhouse collects large amounts of solar energy during the day but gets very cold at night. With all the glass and no insulation, it gains and loses lots of heat. During the day, the greenhouse collects so much heat that it may have to be vented to let heat escape. This energy could help keep the greenhouse warm at night, but it is hard to store this excess heat.

If a greenhouse isn't very practical, how can you build a house that takes advantage of solar heating but doesn't get too hot during the day or too cold at night? How much of the south side should be glass? How can you design a house so that it isn't overheated during the summer? Too much heat coming in the windows in the summer means that you need air-conditioners, which are expensive to operate. Is it possible to design a house to collect lots of heat in the winter but little heat in the summer? You can build some models of houses to test your ideas. Think about how

A passive solar house is designed to take advantage of the sun's energy. Sun shining in the southern windows of this home in Tucson, Arizona, heats air that circulates throughout the house.

to collect the energy and then find out whether your hunches work by running experiments.

MATERIALS AND TOOLS

cardboard
tape
scissors
plastic wrap
thermometer
heat lamp

Use cardboard from boxes to build a model house 60 cm by 60 cm by 30 cm high (2 ft by 2 ft by 1 ft high). Tape any joints between the cardboard so air can't flow in or out. Build the house so that it has an open bottom to allow you to put things inside the house. Make sure that the bottom fits on a horizontal surface without any gaps. Placing it on a rug may help.

Use scissors to cut out two windows 8 cm by 8 cm (3 in by 3 in) in one wall. Put plastic wrap over the windows and use tape to hold the plastic wrap in place. Punch a small hole in the roof so you can insert the thermometer about 5 cm (2 in) into the house.

Place a heat lamp about 2 feet from the house so it shines on the house. The lamp should be shining down at a 30° angle to simulate winter, as shown in Figure 16. Measure the temperature in the house and then turn on the heat lamp. Measure the temperature every minute and see how the temperature changes with time. Record the time and temperatures. Keep recording the temperature until the temperature stops increasing.

Now, cut two more 8-cm-by-8-cm windows in the same side of the house and cover these windows with plastic wrap. Record the temperature and then turn on the heat lamp and record the temperature every minute. Does the rate of change of temperature make sense?

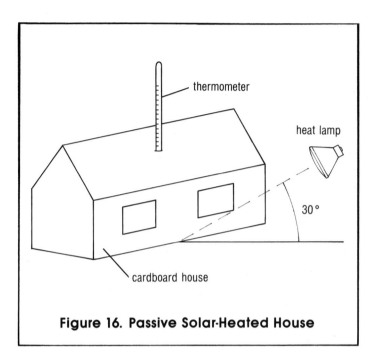

Figure 16. Passive Solar-Heated House

Double the total surface area of the windows again and repeat your measurements. Does the temperature change agree with what you would expect?

**OTHER PROJECTS WITH
PASSIVE SOLAR HOUSES**

1. Modify your experiment by filling a plastic soda bottle with water colored black with food coloring or ink. Place it in the house so that the heat lamp strikes the bottle. See how the temperature of the house changes with time. How does the water affect the temperature change? How can you explain any differences?

2. See what happens to the temperature of the house when the heat lamp is turned off. Test this with and without the bottle of black water. Are the results expected? Does this say something about how to build a passive solar house?

3. Point the heat lamp at an angle of 70° toward the house. This simulates the angle of the sun in summer. See what happens to the temperature of the house, and then build some overhanging eaves to shade the windows. Now, see what happens to the temperature of the house.

4. Design an experiment to see how much more solar heating you get when there is snow on the ground. The snow reflects solar energy off the ground and into the house.

5. Model how a house is affected by solar heating by putting windows on three sides of the house (to represent the east, south, and west), and then find how the temperature varies over time as the heat lamp (sun) moves from east to west during the day. The motion of the heat lamp should be from the horizon to 30° up in the sky to the south of the house and then back to the horizon. Because the sun must go through more atmosphere when near the horizon, you should move the heat lamp farther away from the house when near the horizon to make the test realistic. This will give less heating. Experiment with a house with eaves in the summer as the sun goes from the horizon to 70° and back to the horizon. Repeat the experiment using a heat absorber in the house.

SOLAR HEATING:
TRAPPING THE SUN'S RAYS

Free energy sounds too good to be true. In most cases, it is. An exception is the energy that warms you when you lie in the sun. Sunlight coming into a house through windows is also free energy and helps heat a house in the winter. However, most solar energy is not free because it costs money to build the collector.

Another problem is that solar energy isn't always there. Houses still must be heated on cloudy days. Also, in the winter when you need the most heat, the days are shortest, and the sun is farthest south with the weakest rays. So how can solar energy be collected and used efficiently and economically?

As you think about solar collectors, think about whether they are cost-effective. Do you pay more for the collector and its operation than you would pay for the energy it collects? Can the collector actually be built and used in a real situation? Could your collector be built in developing nations with simple materials and skills? As you run your experiments, think of ways to make your collector more efficient. Can it be made big enough to heat a house, or won't that be economical?

MATERIALS AND TOOLS

two 2-liter soft drink bottles
drill and drill bits
two thermometers
silicone caulk or modeling clay
water
food coloring
aluminum foil

Take the tops off the soda bottles and drill holes in the tops so that thermometers can be inserted in them. Ask an adult to help you with the drilling of these holes.

Now, insert the thermometers into the holes and use the silicone caulk or modeling clay to make a water tight seal between the tops and the thermometers, as shown in Figure 17.

Add water to each bottle and add food coloring to one of them. You want a dark color, so a mix of blue and red would probably be a good choice.

Put on the tops and find the temperature of the water (it should be the same for each bottle). Record these values.

Tall cylinders of water and window
panels made of lexan collect the solar
energy that heats this architect's office.

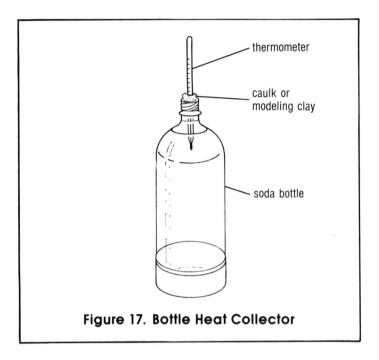

thermometer

caulk or
modeling clay

soda bottle

Figure 17. Bottle Heat Collector

Then place the bottles in the sun for ten minutes and observe the change in temperature of each. Record these
temperatures. Repeat these measurements after another
ten minutes. If the sun is not constant, you will not get good
data.

Next, place aluminum foil behind each bottle so that
sunlight that misses the bottles will be reflected back onto
the bottles. Take your measurements as before. Does using
reflectors make your solar collector more efficient?

**OTHER PROJECTS
WITH SOLAR COLLECTORS**

1. Leave the two bottles from the previous experiment out
in the sun all day, and record the temperature of the water

at regular intervals, say every hour. Plot the temperature versus time on a graph. What happens to the temperature during the day? At night? When is the temperature highest? Lowest? What happens on a cloudy day?

2. Design a collector that uses air as the medium instead of water. Air collectors have an advantage because you don't have to worry about the air freezing. Does making the collector surface black help collect heat?

3. Design a system with a pump that allows water to flow across a collecting area and then stores the water somewhere else. Does this system collect more heat per dollar of investment? Does this system collect more heat? Is it worth the extra cost of a pump?

4. Design a system that uses reflectors to boil water. Be careful because it is possible to design a system that can cause serious burns or eye injuries. Also, make sure that you don't start a fire. Set up your apparatus away from things that can burn and build it out of materials that don't burn.

5. Some solar collectors "track" the sun, meaning they move so that they always get the sun's rays directly on the collector. Design a system that can do this and see how much more heat you gain with the same surface area as a nontracking system. Is it worth the extra cost? Would this kind of system be good for heating a house? What problems might you encounter?

KEEPING HEAT IN WITH INSULATION

Heat is thermal energy or the random motion of molecules. The faster the molecules move, the hotter they are. When molecules give up energy to other molecules, they cool down. To stay warm, you must "insulate," or prevent kinetic energy from escaping.

The construction worker is installing fiberglass insulation to prevent heat from escaping in winter. Insulation conserves energy and reduces heating bills.

But how do you keep heat in? Well, think about what you wear to keep warm in cold weather. The properties of those clothes are probably properties of good insulators. But what happens to insulation in different situations such as when it is very hot or cold or dry or damp? How do you place the insulation to make sure that heat stays in? What happens if there are small cracks in the insulation?

Think about how you keep warm when you go out on a cold day. What do you wear and how do your clothes fit? Why do you sometimes zip up a parka around your neck instead of having it loose? How do you get rid of heat if you are too hot? You keep or lose heat in much the same way houses keep or lose heat. Try experimenting and see whether your ideas, your hypotheses, are correct.

MATERIALS AND TOOLS

cardboard from boxes
scissors
glue and tape
3 thermometers
two 12-oz plastic soda bottles
food wrap

Using cardboard from boxes, build house models about 30 cm by 30 cm by 15 cm tall (1 ft by 1 ft by 6 in tall). Build one with a single layer of cardboard and the other with two layers (twice the insulation). Initially, don't have any windows or doors but leave the bottoms open so that you can place the houses over 12-oz plastic soda bottles. Use tape to hold the houses together, and make a tight seal at any corners or junctions of cardboard. Make sure that the bottoms are flat so that air can't get in at the bottom. Placing them on a rug may help. Punch a hole in each roof with scissors and insert a thermometer so you can measure the temperature inside the house as shown in Figure 18.

Now, fill each soda bottle with hot water from the faucet, as hot as you can get it, being careful not to burn yourself. Measure the temperature with the third thermometer, and then put the tops on tightly. Record the temperature of the water (it should be the same for both).

Next, place a bottle inside each house. Record the highest temperature that occurs inside each house as well as the temperatures at ten-minute intervals for thirty min-

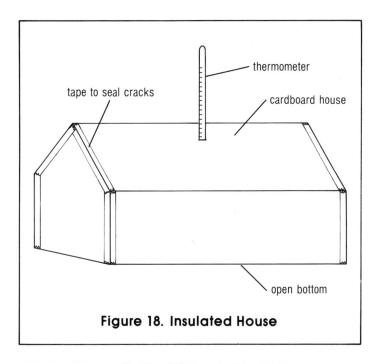

Figure 18. Insulated House

utes. Make sure your data includes all the needed information: which house, what time, what temperature, whether there are windows and doors, and so forth.

Now, cut some windows and a door in each house and repeat your experiment, making sure that the water in the soda bottles is at the same temperature as in the first trial. What do you think will happen to the temperatures when there are open doors and windows? Is your hunch correct?

Next, use the food wrap and tape to cover the windows and doors. Repeat your experiment and record the results. Then, with the windows still taped, build a chimney so that air can flow up the chimney. Leave the door open a small amount and repeat your experiment. What do you think will happen now? Are the results what you expected?

OTHER PROJECTS
WITH INSULATION

1. Add insulation to the house on one layer of cardboard using either fiberglass insulation or styrofoam. Cover any cracks with tape. If you use fiberglass, wear gloves and proper eyewear so that you don't get the glass fibers in your skin or eyes. Start with a thin layer of insulation, 1 cm (½ in) or so, and then double it and see what changes occur. Don't put insulation over the windows because people wouldn't be able to see out. How does the temperature at the end of thirty minutes compare to the other trials? See what happens when you have that kind of insulation but leave the door open and the chimney open.

2. Some types of insulation lose the ability to keep heat in when they are wet. Experiment to see what happens when different kinds of insulation are wet. How does it change their insulating properties? Try materials that keep people warm in clothing or sleeping bags. Do these keep the house warm?

3. Find two houses that are similar in size and number of windows but have different insulation. Find how much heat is needed to keep them warm during the heating season. Does the amount of heat used agree with your experiments?

STORING HEAT FROM
SOLAR COLLECTORS

Solar energy is free, but you can't always collect it, since the sun goes down at night and clouds prevent sunlight from reaching your collector. So how does a solar heating system save heat for times when the sun doesn't shine? What is the most efficient system? Can it be built cheaply?

Most people need a dependable system for their heating. Also, if the costs of installation and upkeep are high, then you don't save much money. You also need a system that is easy to use or you won't use it.

If you are looking for an inexpensive storage system, think about what things are cheap. Air and water are quite cheap. Rocks are also pretty cheap. If a pound of gold could store more heat energy than a pound of rock, it still might be cheaper to use the rock! But what is the best system? How can you efficiently store solar energy for nighttime and cloudy days? Think about how different materials might store heat and then test your hunches.

MATERIALS AND TOOLS

    cardboard boxes
    clear plastic sheet
    black sheet of paper, plastic, or painted material
    tape
    small fan
    scissors
    thermometer
    20 bricks
    20 12-oz soda cans

Get a cardboard box that is about 20 cm (8 in) tall and is 60 cm on each side (2 ft square). Cut off the top and place a black surface on the bottom. This black surface can be black paper, black plastic, or something painted black to act as a heat absorber for the solar collector.

Now, cover the box with clear plastic. Use tape to secure the plastic to the box (even food wrap can be made to work). Then cut a hole with scissors in the side of the box so you can attach a small fan that will blow air into the box. Cut a similar hole in the other side of the box for the air to exit.

Next, take another cardboard box that is large enough to hold 20 bricks or 20 soda cans. Cut a hole in it so you can connect it to the first box such that air exiting the first enters the second box, as shown in Figure 19. Make sure all the air leaving the first box enters the second by using tape to connect the boxes. Cut another hole in the second box at the far side from the first hole to let air escape.

You should be able to put things in the second box and take them out. You can use tape to seal the box after you put them in. Punch a small hole in the side of the big box and insert the thermometer, taping it securely in place.

Now, place both boxes in the sun and turn on the fan. Record the initial temperature and the temperature at two minute intervals until the temperature in the big box doesn't change much. Now, shade the boxes from the sun and place them in the shade and record the temperature every two minutes. How does the temperature change with time in each situation?

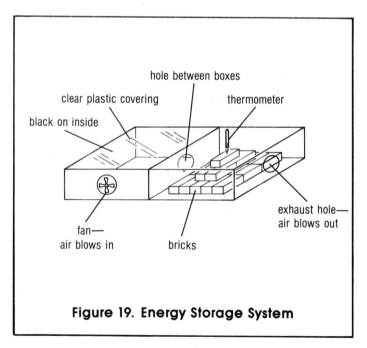

Figure 19. Energy Storage System

Next, place the bricks in the big box so that air can flow past them. The bricks should have as much surface exposed to the air as possible. It is best if they can all be placed in the box without touching each other.

Again, with the system in the sun, turn on the fan, and record the temperatures at two minute intervals. Are the results as you would expect? Then, shade the boxes from the sun and measure the temperature change. Do you expect these results?

Finally, fill the soda cans with water and place them in the box (after you remove the bricks). Repeat your measurements in the sun and in the shade, being careful not to spill the water. Do the results make sense? What seems to be the best way to store heat: air, brick, or water?

OTHER PROJECTS
WITH STORING HEAT

1. Try storing heat in other materials and see whether they store heat more efficiently. How about using plastic soda bottles instead of cans? Make sure that your materials are not hazardous. Ask an adult whether they are safe.

2. Try different geometric arrangements of bricks. Place the bricks as a solid mass and then arrange them so that most surfaces are exposed to the air. What differences do you find?

3. Try storing heat using water in a radiator system. Get a radiator from a car and see whether it stores heat more quickly than cans of water alone. Can you design a system in which water is heated in the radiator and then moved to an attached storage container? Maybe you can have the hot water rise into the container and have cold water sink down to the collector in a "convection" system.

4. Build a model of a solar house with a heat storage system. Find out whether the storage system can even out the temperature in the house and make it more comfortable during the day and night.

CHARACTERISTICS OF LIGHT AND THE ENVIRONMENT

Light is a wonderful thing: it allows us to see, it colors our world, and it can help identify substances. Light waves have different wavelengths: red waves are longer than blue waves. Different substances absorb or reflect different colors. Red paint reflects red light to our eyes, and a red filter allows only red light to get through to our eyes. We see red in both cases. But light can give a scientist more information and may allow identification of the actual substance that is giving off the light or absorbing the light.

But how can light be used to identify a substance? With a bit of experimenting, you can learn more about light and how scientists can detect substances with devices called spectroscopes. Maybe you can design a system to identify pollution or other substances in the air.

You can experiment with a spectroscope, which separates light into its different wavelengths or its *spectra*. Running this experiment will show you that light coming through different substances has a characteristic spectrum. For example, ozone absorbs ultraviolet radiation from the sun, so it acts as a filter. Knowing the wavelengths that are absorbed, you can identify the material doing the absorbing. But how does that help in preserving the environment? Well, it is possible to shine a light through air and find what materials are in it. If you know what is in the air, then you can take steps to correct any problems. It is also possible to identify substances in remote objects like stars just by looking at the wavelengths of light that reach the Earth.

MATERIALS AND TOOLS

    spectroscope
    tape

color filters (available from theater groups)
flashlight

The spectroscope may be difficult to get but is generally available in most high school science departments. Some inexpensive ones are available from a science supply house such as Science Kit, 777 East Park Drive, Tonawanda, NY, 14150 for about $15. While these are not professional quality, they can be used for this type of experiment.

Tape a colored filter over the front of a flashlight. Then, in a darkened room, set the flashlight on a table and from another table look through your spectroscope at the light, as shown in Figure 20. Observe where the bands of light are and record your observations. If your spectroscope has numbers on it, the numbers tell the wavelength of the light.

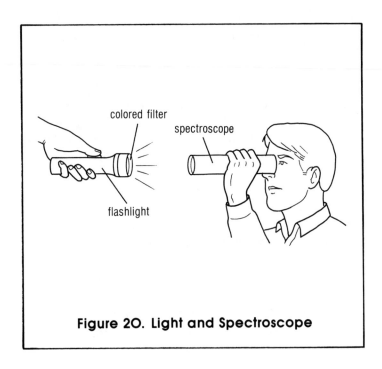

Figure 20. Light and Spectroscope

Record these values and indicate the filter that you are using.

Repeat this with the other color filters that you have. What differences do you observe for the different filters? Could you identify a particular filter by its spectrum? Does the spectrum that you see relate to the color that you see? Do some wavelengths of light coming through the filter surprise you?

OTHER PROJECTS WITH LIGHT

1. Pass the light through different liquids instead of filters. Make sure that the liquids you use are not dangerous. Before you make your observations, see what the spectrum is for the liquid container without the liquid. It may absorb some wavelengths (and leave black lines) so the substance in the container may not be responsible for all the absorption. Can you identify any substances in the container just from the spectrum? Realize that the spectrum of some substances may be hard to see.

2. Design a way to observe the spectrum of the sun without damaging your eyes. Use a very thin slit that allows only a very small amount of light to strike a prism. This light leaving the prism should then fall on a white sheet of paper. *Do not* look directly at the sun, because it can harm your eyes.

3. If particular pollutants absorb particular wavelengths of light, design a system that will allow you to identify when those pollutants are at high concentrations. Some systems are now identifying cars that give out large quantities of pollution in their exhaust. Can you design a similar system?

4. Investigate which wavelengths of light are absorbed by various gases in the atmosphere. Carbon dioxide absorbs infrared light, so it traps heat. What other pollution-related gases do the same thing?

OTHER PROJECTS WITH
ENVIRONMENTAL ENGINEERING

1. Design a system that will prevent erosion when the ground has been disturbed. Land is disturbed during construction or farming, and then the wind blows or the rains come and carry soil away. Losing the dirt is a problem because it clogs the rivers or dirties the air. What kinds of systems can you design to prevent this kind of erosion?

2. Radon gas is a colorless, odorless, naturally occurring gas. Since it is radioactive, however, it is dangerous because it decays into other radioactive atoms. It gets into houses through cracks in the foundation, especially during the heating season, when hot air goes up the chimney and must be replaced somehow. Read about the radon gas problem and then design a system that will keep the gas out of a house. Build a model of your system and test it.

3. If your house uses electric heat, make a study of outside temperature and how much energy your house uses. You might want to use the number of "degree days", the value utilities use to gauge temperature. It is equal to 65° minus the average of the high and low temperatures for a given day. You might also want to take into consideration wind and the amount of sun shining on the house.

4. Make a study of air temperature, amount of sunshine, wind, and water temperature at a lake or pond. Can you predict what will happen to the water temperature at a given windspeed and air temperature?

5. Make a study of the air temperature in a house during warm weather when fans are used to cool it. Place the fans in different places and see what cooling effects you get. What places are most efficient and practical?

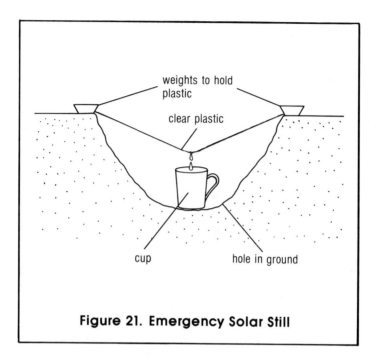

Figure 21. Emergency Solar Still

6. Make a study of how much sunlight falls on your house during a period of time. You might want to design a system with a photoelectric cell that will record the data automatically. Compare the amount of sunlight your house receives to the amount that a local weather station records. What might explain the differences?

7. Design a system to recycle cans in your home or school more easily. Many times, the reason people don't recycle is that it is not convenient or practical. Can you design a system that solves these problems? Remember, each home and school have their own particular problems, and the solution may be different for each place.

8. Design a solar food dryer. You will need a reflector, a drying area that could be made out of a piece of black stovepipe, and a door with vents so that the air can get into the stovepipe and dry the food.

9. Analyze how different kinds of kites fly, and then design and build one of your own and see how it flies. Kites use free energy.

10. Build a "survival still" by putting a piece of plastic in a cone shape across a hole in the ground and letting the sun shine on it. If you place a cup under the bottom of the cone as in Figure 21, you will collect water. What factors affect how much water you collect?

11. Try making adobe bricks out of sand, clay, water, and straw, and then build a structure with them. What combinations of the raw materials work best? How long do you need to let them dry? How can you protect the bricks from water to keep them strong? What do you have to take into account to build with this material? How do they behave like bricks, and how are they different? Where might this cheap building material be useful?

5

WEATHER, ROBOTS, AND REMOTE SENSING

Weather affects our lives on a day-to-day basis. Some weather we think of as good and other as bad, but not all people agree on what is good or bad. Many people think a snowstorm is terrible, but people who live in ski resorts think snow is great. There is a phrase in New England, "If you don't like the weather, wait a minute." Some other areas of the country have more constant weather, but it is important to be able to predict when it will change. How can you predict how hot it is going to be or whether it will rain or snow or be windy?

Much of the data that weather forecasters use comes from distant places. Often the information comes from what are called remote sensors because it is difficult or inconvenient for humans to get the data. Weather balloons carry instruments aloft, satellites fly overhead, and weather buoys float in the ocean. They all radio their instrument readings back to weather forecasting computers.

Remote sensing devices gather information at distant places, while other devices can do tasks by themselves.

Generally, a "robot" is a machine that moves around and does things. Robots are used in nuclear power plants to do tasks where humans don't want to go because of radiation. Robots also do repetitive, boring tasks in assembly lines. Although they don't move like robots, many devices behave as robots and do things at our command. These devices range from the computer, which finds the proper files and sends them to a printer, to the little machine in your car that puts exactly the right amount of gasoline into the cylinders when it is needed.

A number of experiments can be done to understand weather better and to learn how things can be done remotely, perhaps even with robots. Some engineers work on these problems and try to make better weather predictions or better robots. Some readers of this book may be interested in working with weather-related experiments, while others may want to try to build robots. Whatever you do, have fun and learn things along the way.

As you look through the experiments that follow, realize that these are only the beginning of what you might do. Once you perform the initial experiment, you may develop new questions and design new experiments to answer them. Applying science to help society makes a lot of engineers feel good about what they do. You may not solve a large problem, but sometimes little bits fit into the bigger picture. Develop your hypotheses, run experiments to test them, and draw conclusions. It may be that you can help find some of the answers to today's problems. It also may be that you find running experiments so enjoyable that you will make it a career.

DEW POINT AND CLOUDS

Clouds form because the air temperature goes below what is called the *dew point*. As you might guess, the dew point is the temperature at which dew, or small drops of water, starts to form. But what affects the dew point and how does the dew point affect where clouds form? Running some experiments may help you understand dew formation, and you will also learn a bit about the weather in the process.

But how can you make dew form when you want it? Well, dew normally forms at night when it gets cooler, so you might get dew to form by lowering the air temperature. But what temperatures are needed? Are they the same every day? What does humidity have to do with the dew point?

Think about what you know about dew and clouds and try to answer these questions. You might also think about what happens to a glass of ice water. Does dew form on the outside? Does it always form or just sometimes?

MATERIALS AND TOOLS

  glass
  water
  thermometer filled with red liquid
  ice cubes
  old rag
  hammer

Fill a glass about two-thirds full of water and measure its temperature. Use a thermometer with red liquid, *not* a mercury-filled one. Record the temperature.

Now, take some ice cubes, fold them up inside an old rag, and then hit it with a hammer to get some small pieces of ice, as shown in Figure 22. Make sure that you do this on a surface that can't be damaged by a hammer or melted water from the ice.

Add small bits of ice to the water and *gently* stir the ice water mixture with the thermometer, taking care not to break the thermometer. Measure the temperature of the water and notice whether there is any "dew" or water drops forming on the outside of the glass. Slowly add ice and measure the temperature until drops start forming. They

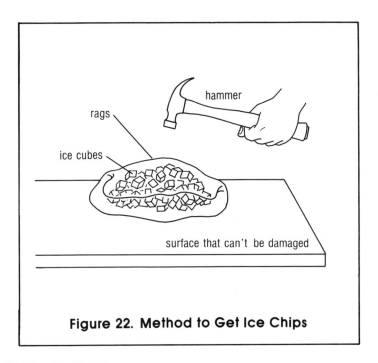

rags

hammer

ice cubes

surface that can't be damaged

Figure 22. Method to Get Ice Chips

may be very small at first so look carefully. Record the temperature when the "dew" starts to form. Also record the type of day it is and where you ran the experiment, inside, outside, or wherever.

Now, repeat your experiment in the bathroom after someone has taken a hot shower. You may have to start with warm water, because even objects at room temperature may have dew form on them. Record the temperature when dew forms and the conditions where you ran your experiment.

Run your experiment on different days and in different places. During the heating season, run your experiment inside and outside to observe differences. This will not work when the temperature is near or below freezing outside, because the air must be cooled below the freezing point of water. Then "frost" will form.

Develop a hypothesis to explain your data. Then try to predict the temperature at which dew will form in a new situation. The dew point generally changes as storms pass by. Measure the dew point outside before a storm, during it, and after it passes by.

OTHER PROJECTS WITH DEW POINT AND CLOUDS

1. As air rises, it expands and cools. As the temperature drops, clouds form as the "dew point" is reached. In clouds, water condenses on small particles in the air instead of on the outside of the glass or on the ground. Make observations about clouds and estimate the height of the cloud bottoms, the point where dew starts to form. It may be difficult to get exact measurements of cloud altitude, but you can estimate it as high, medium, or low. The height at which clouds form may change during the day so make your measurements more than once. Make a study of the dew point measured on the ground, the air temperature, and the cloud heights. Does there seem to be a pattern? You may be able to get precise cloud heights from The Weather Channel.

2. Run an experiment with a closed container such as a gallon plastic milk jug into which you can insert a glass and a medicine dropper as in Figure 23. The glass should be open at the top but the container should fit tightly around it. Place the container in a freezer (where there is very little water vapor). After the container has been there for an hour or so, carefully knock out any frost that has formed inside. Repeat the process and then while the container still has *cold* air in it, insert the glass. You can then seal the container after you take it into a warm room. If the container expands too much as the temperature of the air rises, you may have to make a pinhole to relieve the inside pressure.

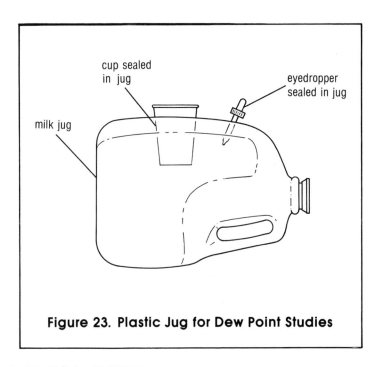

milk jug

cup sealed
in jug

eyedropper
sealed in jug

Figure 23. Plastic Jug for Dew Point Studies

Now, add 0.5 cubic centimeter (cm³) of water with the medicine dropper to the container. Shake the container and then let it sit for 10 minutes or so. Then add water and ice to the glass to find the temperature when dew forms. You can see the dew form by looking through the glass. Dew may not form even at 0°C initially. Remove the ice water from the glass, add another 0.5 cm³ of water, shake the container, wait 10 minutes for the water to evaporate, and then find the dew point. Record the temperature and the amount of water added to the container. Keep adding water until the dew point is at room temperature. What is the relationship between the amount of water in the air and the dew point? What might happen if the temperature rises more? Run your experiment on a hot day. Are your results expected?

3. Sometimes weather forecasters talk about the comfort index, which is a combination of heat and amount of moisture in the air. Make your own scale using temperature and dew point. See how it agrees with the weather forecaster's.

HEATING AND COOLING
WITH CHANGES OF STATE

A change of state occurs when something changes from solid to liquid (melts) or liquid to gas (vaporizes), or the reverse, which is freezing or condensing. Molecular bonds are broken during melting or vaporization, and energy must be used to break the bonds. The heat must come from somewhere. After swimming on a windy day, water evaporates from your skin. You get cool because the water molecules need energy to break their bonds and *you* give it to them (brrrr). Ice keeps drinks cold because solid bonds are broken as ice melts and the energy to break the bonds comes from the drink.

But what happens when the reverse of melting or vaporizing happens? When something freezes (goes from the liquid to the solid) or condenses (goes from gas to liquid) heat is given off instead of absorbed. Something is heated. Steam heating systems use the "heat of condensation" by sending steam into radiators. As the steam condenses, it gives off heat. The water then drains back down the pipe to be turned back into steam in the boiler.

But how much heat is gained or lost during a change of state? How can systems be built to use this heat gain or loss? Could you engineer a refrigerator or air conditioner to operate on this principle? What other devices could you design to take advantage of a change of state?

MATERIALS AND TOOLS

    rags
    string

thermometer
water
clamp
fan

Take the rags and roll them into a long cylinder about 5 cm (2 in) in diameter. Use the string to tie the rags. Insert the thermometer into the center of the cylinder. Soak the rag cyclinder with hot water from a faucet, and clamp it so it stands upright as in Figure 24. Read the temperature on the thermometer and record this value.

Now, turn on the fan so it blows at the rags. Find how long it takes for the temperature to drop 1 degree. Keep the rags constantly wet. Try to predict how the temperature will change, and then see whether your predictions are

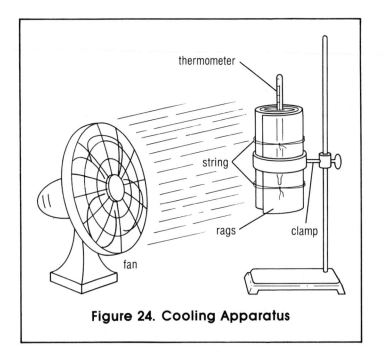

Figure 24. Cooling Apparatus

correct. Stop your experiment if the temperature becomes constant. The temperature change may be slow, so be patient.

OTHER PROJECTS
WITH CHANGES OF STATE

1. Run your experiment on different days and see whether the temperature changes in different ways. With different amounts of humidity, your results may vary. Try to predict the differences and then experiment to find out whether your predictions are correct. You might also try running your experiment in the bathroom after someone has taken a hot shower. Be careful to keep the fan away from water.

2. Design an experiment to see whether the rags wrapped around a bottle of water can cool the water (a quart plastic milk bottle works well). Measure the amount of water you place on the rag, and see whether adding twice the water causes twice the cooling.

3. Run experiments to find how many grams of water can be cooled 1 degree with one gram (1 g) of melting ice.

4. Design a system of tubing to build an air conditioner that uses evaporation. Air from the room must go into the tubing, be cooled, and then come back out to the room. The air in the room should be separate from the air that evaporates the water from cloth; the room would be un-comfortable if too much water vapor were added to it, because it would increase the humidity.

WIND SPEED INDICATORS:
SIMPLE AND HIGH TECH

Measuring wind speed is important for many people. Of course, weather forecasters need to know wind speed to make weather forecasts. But other people need to know wind speed, and they measure it in different ways. Pilots use wind socks, sailors use wave size, and farmers use the motion of plants and trees. Some methods are more precise than others. But how do these different indicators work? Can you build an inexpensive one that is accurate?

Wind speed indicators work because the wind has energy, which can move something to give a reading. But how can you build something that gives repeatable readings? In order for your device to be of any use, the results must be repeatable. So what kind of device can you build?

As you think about wind speed indicators, think about what happens to familiar objects when the wind blows. Then develop a hypothesis as to what will happen with something you build and test your hypothesis.

MATERIALS AND TOOLS

saw
thin plywood, ⅛ in (3 mm) thick
1 x 3 in (2.5 cm x 7.6 cm) board
dowel or broomstick ¾ in (2 cm) in diameter or
    larger
duct tape
screw and screw driver
marker
protractor
car, driver, and untraveled road

With a saw, cut two pieces of plywood, one 5 cm by 15 cm (2 in by 6 in) and the other 20 cm by 20 cm (8 in by 8 in). Cut a 15-cm-long (6-in-long) piece of 1 × 3. *Be careful when you use the saw, and get an adult to help you.* Keep your hands clear of the area that you are sawing.

Check the dowel and if one end is not square, cut it so it is. (If you are using a broomstick, cut the end you hold so you can still screw it into a broom after you are finished experimenting.)

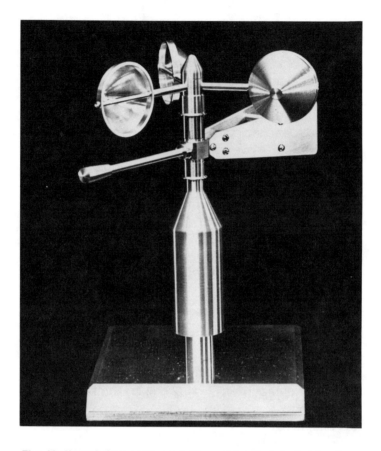

The National Oceanic and Atmospheric Administration uses cup-type anemometers like this one. The three cups measure wind speed, and the wind vane measures wind direction.

Next, take a piece of duct tape about 25 cm (10 in) long. Stick 8 mm (3 in) of it to one end of the smaller piece of plywood and leave the rest hanging off. Next, take another piece of duct tape 10 cm (4 in) long and stick it to the sticky side of the first piece of tape next to the plywood as shown in Figure 25. This will make the center 10 cm of the 25-cm section of tape *not* sticky. Then, wrap this part of the tape around the dowel and stick the sticky part of the tape to the opposite side of the plywood. The plywood should now swing freely, but still be attached to the dowel.

Remove the plywood from the dowel (it should just slip off) and repeat the taping procedure for the 6-inch piece of 1 × 3. Now you have two different pieces of wood that can swing easily on the dowel.

Next, take the larger piece of plywood and attach it with a screw to the end of the dowel, as shown in Figure 26. Use the marker to make lines at 10° intervals as shown. Label these angles.

Now, it is time to experiment and see how wind speed is related to how much the wood swings. Take your appara-

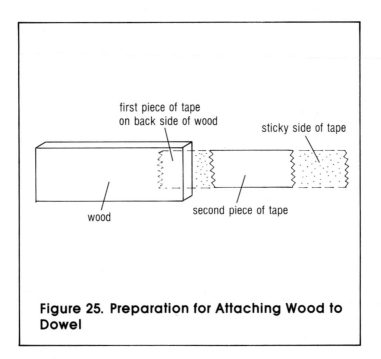

Figure 25. Preparation for Attaching Wood to Dowel

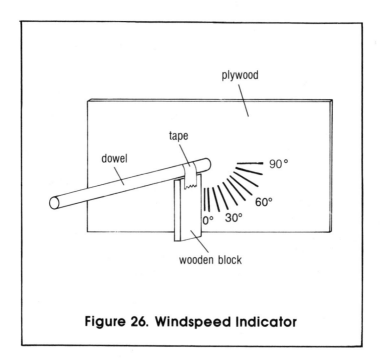

Figure 26. Windspeed Indicator

tus to an untraveled road and have a driver drive you at different constant speeds. This can be dangerous if other cars are on the road. Use common sense and obey all laws. Also, when you stick anything out of a window, make sure that you don't hit anything. It could hurt you or the things (or people) you hit.

Stick the dowel out of the car parallel to the road with 0° pointing down. Start with the plywood on the dowel. Have the driver drive at 5 mph, then 10 mph, then 15 mph, and so on, up to 40 mph (8,16, 24, and 64 km/hr). Do not drive faster than 40 mph because it is dangerous to have something out the window at speeds above this. It is also rare to have actual wind speeds higher than 40 mph. Record the angle to which the plywood swings and the speed of the car. Repeat your measurements when the 1 × 3 is on the dowel. You can now tell wind speed by measuring the angle. You may want to mark the wind speeds on the plywood. What do you expect your results to be? Are the results what you predict?

OTHER PROJECTS WITH
WIND SPEED INDICATORS

1. As the car moves through the air, it displaces air. This means that the flow of air past the car is not uniform. Try running your experiment with the swinging plywood 60 cm (2 ft) from the car, 30 cm (1 ft) from the car, and right beside the car. What differences do you detect? What might be the reason for the differences?

2. Use different pieces of wood or material to measure slower wind speeds. Is it possible to get a device that can accurately measure speeds between 0 and 2 mph (0 and 3 km/r)? Often, this kind of sensor is important for finding air leaks. In the wintertime, air often leaks into a house around doors. You can use a wind speed indicator to measure how much cold air comes in. Perhaps you can show how much less cold air comes in after weather stripping is applied to seal the cracks.

3. Nature provides many wind speed indicators when leaves are on the trees. Can you develop a wind scale using the leaves and trees? Use the wind speed indicator you built to measure wind speeds and record your observations.

4. Build a wind sock like those at an airport or use one you buy in a store. Make a chart that relates the wind speed to the way the wind sock behaves.

5. Use your wind speed indicator to relate wave size on a pond to the wind speed. Remember, waves get larger if the wind blows for a longer distance. Wave heights may be different for a given wind speed if the wind direction is different.

6. Build a cup wind speed indicator similar to the ones used by weather observatories. You can attach the cup system to a small DC motor that will generate a current when turned. (Motors are just generators run the opposite way.) Connect the wires from the motor to an ammeter and measure the current. Use your wind speed indicator to find how current relates to wind speed.

7. You can also make a wind speed indicator out of a DC fan attached to an ammeter. When the fan spins, it will generate a current that increases with wind speed.

LIGHT-EMITTING DIODES (LEDs) AND TRANSISTORS

Electronic circuits are found in everything from cars to stereos to computers. But how do they work and what do they do? Most people have heard of transistors, but how do they function in a stereo and why are they so useful? Computer chips are electronic circuits that have millions of transistors working together. While you can work with a computer without knowing how transistors work, it may be fun to know a little bit about how they behave.

Basically, a transistor acts as a switch, and running experiments with transistors can show you how they work. These experiments are quite simple but you can learn some basic electronics from them. Other experiments may become quite involved, and to carry them out, you will have to learn more about electronics than this small section covers. However, if you don't know much about electronics, it is best to start with simple things and then work up to more complex ones.

As you do these simple experiments, think about how

they might apply to a stereo system or even a computer. Computers are rather dumb and really have only a lot of switches that are either on or off. Can you build such a simple switch? Is it possible for you to build simple computer logic circuits? Can you figure out what the circuit elements are doing?

MATERIALS AND TOOLS

goggles or glasses
wires
4 1½-volt batteries
battery holder for four batteries (to give 6 volts'
  output)
1,000 ohm (Ω) resistors
diode (1N914)
light-emitting diode (LED)
switch (that can send current from center to either
  side)
NPN transistor (2N2222)
PNP transistor (2N2907)
3,000 Ω resistor
9-volt power source

NOTE: These materials can be purchased at an electronics store such as Radio Shack.

Follow these directions carefully and make sure that you pay attention to the warnings. The circuit elements can heat up and explode. *Do not connect a wire from one end of the battery directly to the other.* Also, *do not connect the battery directly to a light-emitting diode. Always* wear *goggles* or *glasses* in case something explodes.

Connect a circuit similar to the one shown in Figure 27, but leave the switch *open,* meaning that electricity cannot go through the switch. Generally the switch handle is up in this position. The leads can be twisted together or mounted on a circuit board. Make sure the light-emitting diode and

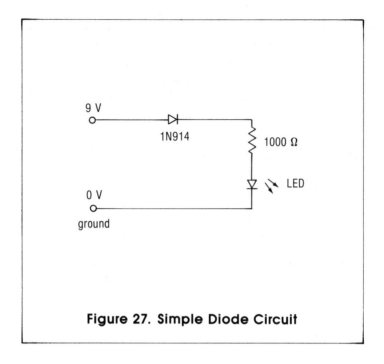

9 V

1N914

1000 Ω

0 V

ground

LED

Figure 27. Simple Diode Circuit

regular diode are connected with the proper polarity. After you have checked your circuit, close the switch. What do you observe? Record your observations.

Now, open the switch, turn the normal diode around in the circuit, and then close the switch. What do you observe? Record your results. What does a diode seem to do?

Next, set up a circuit so that it is similar to Figure 28. Leave the switch *open* until you have checked your circuit. When you are sure that it is correct, see what happens when you move the switch from position #1 to #0. Record the results.

Now, build the circuit shown in Figure 29. Switch the switch to the different positions. Record your results.

What have these three simple experiments shown you about diodes and transistors? How does the voltage + or

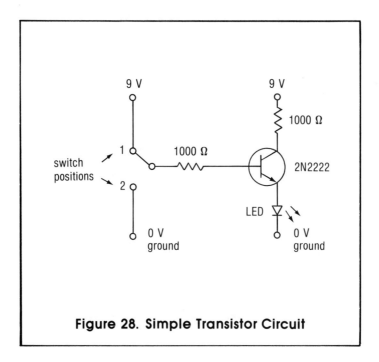

Figure 28. Simple Transistor Circuit

— affect the current flow? Does the lighting of the LED occur when you expect it? Make a list of your observations and then try to make a theory about how the circuits work.

Replace the NPN transistor with a PNP transistor (2N2907). What differences do you observe? "P" material has positive charge carriers and "N" material has negative charge carriers. A "PNP" transistor has "N" material between layers of "P" material.

OTHER PROJECTS WITH LEDs AND TRANSISTORS

NOTE: LEDs can have only a little current go through them. With too much, they explode. Whenever you use an LED, you must have at least 1,000 ohms (Ω) of resistance in the

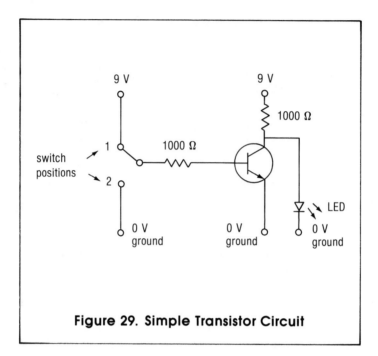

Figure 29. Simple Transistor Circuit

circuit. When current leaves the battery, it must go through 1,000 Ω of resistance, through the LED (plus other circuit parts like switches or transistors), and then back to the battery. Wear either goggles or glasses for protection.

1. Build a circuit with two transistors, one of each kind, and see what voltages make the LED light up. The output from the first transistor should go into the base, or middle connection, of the second transistor as shown in Figure 30.

2. Build the circuits shown in Figure 31 with diodes, resistors, and LEDs to experiment with computer logic. Computer logic uses OR (A or B), NOR (not A or B), AND (both A and B), and NAND (not A and B). Connect each circuit and observe whether the LED lights when you have nothing

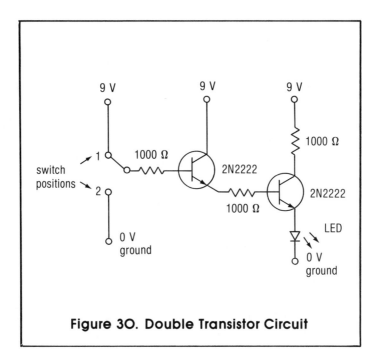

Figure 3O. Double Transistor Circuit

connected to A or B. Then test what happens when you connect positive 6 volts to A or B or both. Which circuit is OR? NOR? AND? NAND?

3. Find a circuit diagram for a simple radio or other simple electronic device and try to figure out what the transistors do. You may have to find some other books about electronics in the library to help you, or you may be able to ask your teacher or someone who works with electronics.

ROBOTS AND REPETITIVE TASKS

Robots summon visions of heroes like R2D2 but robots come in many forms. Most robots do tasks that humans normally do; some may even look like humans. Often, these hu-

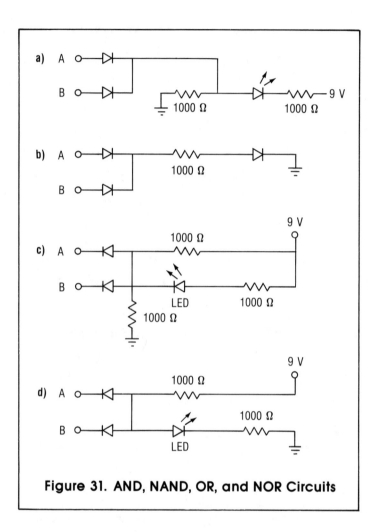

a) A ○—▷|
   B ○—▷| ⎓ 1000 Ω   ▷| ╱╱ —ww— 9 V
                                        1000 Ω

b) A ○—▷| —ww— —▷|
              1000 Ω
   B ○—▷|

                                    9 V
              1000 Ω   ○
c) A ○—◁| —ww—
   B ○—◁| ◁| LED   —ww—
                        1000 Ω
         ⌇ 1000 Ω

                                    9 V
              1000 Ω   ○
d) A ○—◁| —ww—
                      1000 Ω
   B ○—◁| ▷| —ww—
              LED

Figure 31. AND, NAND, OR, and NOR Circuits

manlike robots are just built that way to make them more friendly or perhaps just to be cute. But what can robots actually do? Can they make decisions? How are they designed?

Some robots can be quite simple, while other projects with robots will consume a lifetime. The complexity of the

**This robot carries trays of food
to patients in a hospital.**

robot is related to the task it is meant to do. People who fly radio controlled planes are actually flying a robot. They command the robot, a series of electric motors, to move controls and fly the plane. Robots also work on the assembly line doing repetitive tasks and can be programmed to be more precise than humans can be. Robots also can work in places where humans can't work safely, for instance, in areas of nuclear power plants with high radiation levels.

But how can you start building robots? Well, starting with a simple project is best. But what project is simple enough? How can the simple project turn into a more complex one? Is it easy to hook up computer controls to the robot? How can a robot make "decisions" about what to do and when to do it? Robots apply technology to solve a problem. Motors, sensors, and control systems in robots are not new; they are just put together in new ways. No one has a monopoly on new ways to do things. Think about what you want a robot to do and then build one. The initial experiment in this section may hardly look or work like a "robot." However, if you make the strings move by electric motors and add some remote sensors to "see" when the task needs to be done, then instead of a human doing the work, the robot would do it all by itself.

MATERIALS AND TOOLS

½ in (1.3 cm) plywood
1-in-by-1-in (2.5 by 2.5-cm) wood sticks
drill
5 cm (2-in)-long round-headed bolts with nuts
string
screw eyes
marker
soda cans

Build a system on the plywood similar to the one in Figure 32. Drill holes in the wood sticks large enough for the bolts

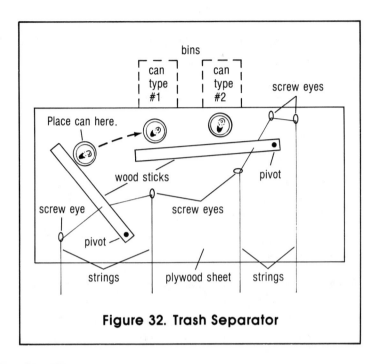

Figure 32. Trash Separator

to go through as an axis. Drill similar holes in the plywood where you want the axis to be. Now, push the bolts up through the plywood and then through the wooden sticks. Put nuts on the bolts, but be careful not to tighten them too much because the wood sticks have to move. Tie string either directly to the sticks or to the screw eyes as shown. Use the marker to label the positions as shown in Figure 32.

The system uses a lever to move a soda can from where it is placed to a position where another lever can push the can into the proper place for recycling. This "robot" needs the help of a human to pull the strings and to "sense" where each can needs to be moved.

Use your system to sort different types of cans, and then think of how you can modify it. Can you make a system that will deliver the cans to the plywood rather than having someone place them there? Can you use electric motors to replace your pulling the strings? Can you replace the strings with motors that are directly attached to the wood sticks? Can you design a sensor that would identify which can is which so it can be sorted?

OTHER PROJECTS WITH ROBOTS AND REPETITIVE TASKS

1. Erector Sets and Legos have motors and parts that can move. Use these materials to build robots that are more complex and can do different tasks. Think of something that you want the robot to do, and then design a robot that will do it.

2. Most robots use computer controls to program the robot to do particular tasks. In a factory, the robot would be programmed to move its arm to the right, then forward, weld along a particular line, and then move the arm back to the original position. Computer-controlled systems can operate without humans and can do repetitive tasks without getting bored or tired. Design a robot to use computer controls for its motors. You may want to do this completely on your own or use robotic programs available through science supply stores.

Remember, robots can be simple or complex. They can be costly or inexpensive, depending on your designs. Your robot is limited only by your imagination and the time and money you have for your project.

REMOTE SENSING

Sometimes you can gather data by going to the place where you want to gather it, taking it, and returning. But what if you want to gather data about the temperature of lava, the bottom of a lake, the inside of the engine of a car, or perhaps just outside? Remote sensing may help.

Remote sensing uses a machine or device to get data and then relay the information to you. Some systems are quite simple, while others are complex.

The easiest remote sensor to build is one that you can see at a distance like a large thermometer outside a house. The sensor is outside, but it can be read from inside the house. How can other systems work? You obviously can't see inside a car engine when it is running, so how can you measure the temperature inside the cylinders? Can you build a system that relays data from outside to the inside? What kinds of data can you gather?

Once you decide what data you want, design a system that will gather it. You may also want a system to record the data for you so you don't have to be constantly present. But how do you get started? What do you have to build? Do the following simple experiment and you may get some more ideas. Think about the data you would like to know, and then build the apparatus to get them.

MATERIALS AND TOOLS

thermistor
insulated wire
wire stripper
resistor with similar resistance to thermistor's mid-
    range
9-volt battery holder and battery
solder gun and solder
silicone caulk or nail polish
voltmeter
cup for water
hot water
thermometer
ice cubes

Take the thermistor (available at an electronics store), which has a temperature range that includes 0°C to 50°C (32°F to 122°F) and a resistance at room temperature between

A very sophisticated remote sensor is the Hubble
Space Telescope, which takes photographs of objects
in deep space. As it orbits Earth, the telescope is repaired
and maintained by the space shuttle, at lower right.

1,000 and 10,000 Ω. A thermistor decreases its resistance as temperature rises and the change can be rather large. A thermistor with the given values is the easiest to work with but almost any will do.

Remove the insulation from the ends of the wire with a wire stripper, *being careful not to cut yourself.* With the wire, connect the resistor, battery holder, and thermistor as shown in Figure 33. All connections should be soldered if possible. This makes better, more permanent connections. Be careful not to burn yourself or heat the thermistor or resistor too much. Get an adult to help you use the soldering gun. Improper soldering may cause bad results or injuries.

Next, cover the wires from the thermistor and the bare wire attached to it with silicone caulk (nail polish will do) to make the connection waterproof. Set the circuit aside until the caulk dries.

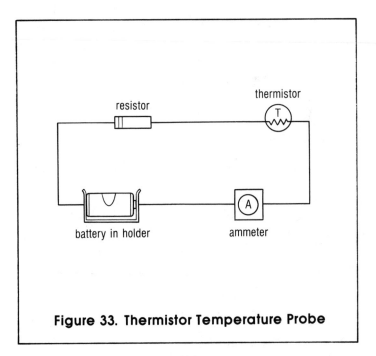

Figure 33. Thermistor Temperature Probe

Now, connect a voltmeter across the resistor and insert the battery into the battery holder. Measure the voltage drop across the resistor; it should be between 1 volt and 8 volts. If you get a voltage in this range, then your circuit is working, and you made good connections.

Now, get a cup and fill it with hot water from the tap and then put the thermistor into the water. (*Remember: You can use only low-voltage electricity around water; 9 volts is OK but household current at 120 volts could kill you.*) Use the thermometer to measure the water temperature. Record the temperature and the voltage drop across the resistor. Now, add a small amount of ice and observe the temperature and voltage. Add more ice in small amounts until the temperature reaches 0°C. Record the temperature and voltage at each point.

Your data shows how voltage corresponds to temperature (as long as your battery is not dead). You can now use your system to measure temperatures in a remote place. If you run the wires outside, you can measure the outside temperature from the inside. (Do not leave the battery on too long because it will run down.) Record the temperature changes during the day. How does your system compare to walking outside to look at the thermometer?

OTHER PROJECTS
WITH REMOTE SENSING

1. If you have access to a lake and a boat, with an adult's permission and proper safety precautions, find how the water temperature in the lake varies with depth. Lower your sensor into the water (you may need a small weight attached to it) and measure the temperature at regular intervals of depth, say 1, 2, 3 meters (3, 6, 9 ft), and so on. You may make this into a longer-term project and measure the temperature at different times during the year.

2. Design a system that allows you to measure wind speed at a remote place. Generally, winds at ground level aren't as fast as they are at treetop level. Design a system with spinning cups so that you can measure the wind speed at a high place from the ground.

3. Flooding often can't be prevented, but people can be warned to move to higher ground. The warning systems generally measure stream flow or the depth of water in streams at different places. Design a system that measures water depth and relays the information to you.

4. Many remote sensing systems relay their information by radio to computers that then store and use the data. Design a system using a computer to get data from a remote place and to store the data.

OTHER PROJECTS WITH WEATHER, ROBOTS, AND REMOTE SENSING

1. Track the paths of hurricanes during hurricane season. Get a map and plot the positions as well as the top wind speed. You may want to plot the hurricanes in the Atlantic or the Pacific Oceans or both.

2. Use a computer to track temperatures outside your house. Look at the patterns of temperature changes in twenty-four-hour periods and longer. How are clouds, wind, and sun related to your temperature variations?

3. Build a weather station that can record temperatures, rainfall, wind, and barometric pressure and use it to help you to predict the weather. You may want to make it similar to the National Weather Forecast stations so you may want to read about those systems. It is possible to build your own rain gauge and barometer for less money than you can buy them.

4. Design and build a system that allows you to measure how much water flows in a stream. You will need to measure the speed of the water at different depths as well as the profile or shape of the channel. If you do this at different times, you can see how the flow rate changes over the year. You can also relate the stream flow to the amount of rainfall.

5. Build a robot that can do things human hands can do. You may want to design one to tie knots or pick up objects. Your robot may be one that uses human power or electric motors and a computer to operate it.

6. Design a system to detect whether people are in the area around your house. These systems can be bought for lots of money; you may be able to build one that costs less. You can start with things such as photodetectors and sound-activated switches, then build a system that meets your needs.

7. If you are in an area with lots of thunderstorms, make a study of the clouds, winds, rain, and amounts of thunder from different storms. Are there any patterns? Can you tell what the storm will be like just by looking at the clouds? The wind?

8. Build some simple weather instruments: a barometer, which measures air pressure, and a hygrometer, which measures humidity. The barometer can be built out of a container with a balloon stretched across it, and the hygrometer can be made with a long hair. The problem with building these devices is that there isn't much motion. Levers are needed to make a large motion out of a small one, as shown in Figure 34.

9. Make observations of clouds, winds, and temperatures, and then see whether the weather seems to follow a pattern associated with them. Does an east wind come before a particular type of weather? What other things can you discover?

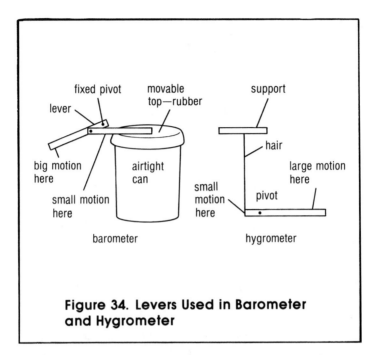

Figure 34. Levers Used in Barometer and Hygrometer

10. Run experiments to see the insulating effect of snow. How does the temperature of something change in a snowdrift as compared to on top of the snow?

6

SCIENCE FAIRS

Entering a science project in a science fair can help you focus on solving a particular problem. Sometimes working toward such a goal forces you to look critically at your project and ask questions about your data and conclusions. "Going public" with your project means that many people will look at your data. They will try to analyze it, and if someone points out a flaw in your reasoning, it is embarrassing. Entering the science fair makes you think hard about what you have done and what you have discovered. It can be hard work but very rewarding.

The judges will look at how you apply scientific principles and how you solve a particular problem. Remember, engineers apply science to the problems that society faces, and this is what you do for science fairs. You may design a better can opener or find a way to reduce or identify pollution. All of these are good projects.

Projects are judged on the basis of originality, presentation, and scientific content. Others may have done projects similar to yours, but yours may have a new viewpoint or method to collect data. You must also demonstrate that you understand your data, and your conclusions should be based on your data and sound scientific principles. You must also express your ideas so others can understand what you did and how you reached the conclusions. If your presentation is unclear, others can't learn from you. Making a clear presentation takes time.

Because your project will be viewed by many people, you must make sure it answers the questions that viewers will ask about your project. You must clearly outline your experiment. You must state what you did, present your data and show how you got it, and include how you reached your conclusions. Preparing for a science fair may seem like a lot of work, but you learn more because you ask yourself hard questions. Does your data really show what you think it does? Is another explanation possible? What are the unanswered questions? Could you be missing an important thought? By using more data could you prove something else?

PRESENTATION

Your project will be viewed by others who want to understand what you have done. Therefore, you must present your ideas clearly and concisely. If they can't quickly understand what you have done and what you are concluding, many people may just walk past. Your presentation should also catch the eye of people. First impressions make a difference, and people may not stop and learn about your project if something doesn't jump out and grab their attention. Make your project look nice, but don't sacrifice science in the process.

Before you start working on the presentation, review your experiment from beginning to end:

1. Think of the original hypothesis and design of your project.

2. Review notes you may have taken on any reading related to your project.

3. Look over your data and observations, noting anything that might seem strange or inconsistent.

4. See whether your graphs and tables make sense.

5. Make sure that your conclusions follow from your data and the data are interpreted correctly.

Once you have thought about the five points mentioned, it is time to start writing. Often writing about your work is not easy. However, if scientists do not publish their discoveries, someone else may have to discover what they already have discovered. Often, once you get started, the writing becomes easier. Some people may find making the presentation is as hard as doing the project. For others, it will be easier.

Your report should be formal with a title page that gives the name of your project, your name, school, address, and the date. The exact way the title page should be written may vary from science fair to science fair. You should also give credit and thanks to the people who helped you or lent you equipment. These people may even want a copy of the paper and want to see your project.

You may have to include a table of contents followed by a statement of the project's purpose, which is a sentence or two about what you were trying to show. An abstract may follow; it is designed to allow a reader to find out quickly what you did and what you concluded. This allows them to look at the project more closely if they desire. A sample abstract follows:

CAPTURING SUNLIGHT WITH INEXPENSIVE MATERIALS
Sol R. Collector
Sunset Lane
Sunhurst, Md.

A study was done with inexpensive materials to see which materials would collect solar energy most effectively. Heat gain was measured by the temperature rise of air in a box measuring 1 meter on each side. The box was insulated and no sunlight struck the box. Air from the collector moved through an insulated air duct. The ability of the different materials to collect solar energy was determined by the temperature change of the air in the box. Seven different systems were tested.

The background section of the report should contain information you found in books and set down the scientific principles used to analyze your data. You should briefly discuss what you have read, and why it is important, and how particular scientific principles apply.

The section discussing the procedure by which you ran the experiment should include a description of the apparatus, generally with photographs and drawings if you can't present the actual apparatus. A person reading your report should be able to tell exactly what you did and why you did it. Make sure to label things clearly.

Your data and conclusions should be presented in a logical and clear form. Graphs and tables may help to present the ideas clearly. If the data is unclear, a reader may miss important information and reach improper conclusions, ones different from yours. If you think errors are possible in some of your data, mention how large they may be. Be realistic so someone doesn't ask you an embarrassing question.

The bibliography finishes the report and is a list of books, articles, and other sources you used for your paper. These should be listed in alphabetical order by author (with the last name first). You should also include the page number if you used specific information rather than just general information from the whole book or article. Often, sample bibliographies are provided by the science fair committee, and you can also look at the bibliography for this book on the following pages.

BIBLIOGRAPHY

Boys, C.V. *Soap Bubbles*. New York: Dover Publications, 1959.

Brisk, M. *1001 Ideas for Science Projects*. New York: Prentice-Hall/Arco, 1992.

Cook, James. *Thomas Edison Book of Easy and Incredible Experiments*. New York: Dodd, Mead & Co., 1988.

Feldman, David. *Why Do Clocks Run Clockwise?*. New York: Harper and Row, 1988.

Goodwin, Peter. *Engineering Projects for Young Scientists*. New York: Franklin Watts, 1987.

———. *Physics Projects for Young Scientists*. New York: Franklin Watts, 1991.

———. *How Everyday Things Work*. Portland, Me.: J. Weston Walch, 1992.

Herbert, Don. *Mr. Wizard's 400 Experiments in Science*. North Bergen, N.J.: Book Lab, 1968.

Landers, Ed. *Secrets of 1 2 3: Classic Science Tricks and Experiments*. Blue Ridge Summit, Pa.: TAB Books/McGraw Hill, 1987.

UNESCO. *700 Science Experiments for Everyone.* New York: Doubleday, 1962.

Walker, Jearl. *The Flying Circus of Physics.* New York: John Wiley and Sons, 1977.

Williams, Jack. *The Weather Book.* New York: Vintage Books, 1992.

INDEX

Automatic shifts, 39–45

Basketballs, spinning,
 34–38
  materials and tools, 36
Bicycles
  and gears, 28–31
  and rolling friction,
   20–23
  streamlining, 49–50
Bridges, 51

Cars, 50
  engine performance,
   31
  and heat energy, 19
  rubber band-powered,
   34

shape of, 50–51
solar-powered, 50
tire pressure and
  rolling friction, 20–22
torque converters,
  39–45
wind speed indicators,
  97
Changes of state, 90–92
Classroom science project,
 14
Clouds and dew point,
 85--90
  materials and tools, 86
  projects, 88–90
Collectors, solar, 66–70
Controls, 17–18
Cooling, 90–92

Data, 16–17
    and changes, 18
    presentation, 117
"Degree days," 81
Dew point and clouds,
    85–90
    materials and tools, 86
    projects, 88–90
Drawing machine, 50

Einstein, Albert, 18
Electricity, 53, 58
Energy, 19–51
    basketballs, 34–38
    bicycles, 28–31, 49–50
    bridges, 51
    defined, 19
    drawing machine, 50
    furniture, 48–49
    gears, 28–31
    heat energy, 19
    jar opener, 50
    raft with paddle
        wheels, 50
    rocking chairs, 45–48
    rubber bands and
        springs, 32–34
    saving, importance of,
        19
    solar-powered car/
        boat, 50
    spinning balls, 34–39
    string trimmers, 23–27
    tire pressure and
        rolling friction, 20–23
    torque converters and

    automatic shifts,
        39–45
    wind tunnel, 50–51
Energy of motion, 36
Engineering, 11–15
Environment, 52–83
    insulation, 70–74
    light, 78–80
    other projects, 81–83
    passive solar-heated
        house, 62–66
    solar-heating, solar
        collectors, 66–70
    store heat from solar
        collector, 74–78
    wave energy, 57–62
    windmills, 53–57
Erosion, 81
Experimenting, 14–15

Failures, 13–14
Food energy, 19
Force equation, 29
Furniture, 45–49

Gears and bicycles, 28–31
    buying gears, 31
    materials and tools, 28
    other projects, 31
Greenhouse, 62

Heat
    changes of state,
        90–92
    condensation, 90
    heat energy, 19

Heat (cont.)
    insulation, 70–74
    solar heating, 62–69
    storing, 74–78
Hoola hoops, 38
Houses, solar heating,
    62–66
    materials and tools, 64
    other projects, 65–66
Hypothesis, 18, 26

Insulation, 70–74
    materials and tools, 72
    other projects, 74

Light, 78–80
    materials and tools,
    78–79
    projects, 79
Light-emitting diodes (LEDs),
    98–103
    materials and tools, 99
    projects, 101–103

Machines, 18
Materials, substitutes, 14
Math requirements, 13
Measurements, 18
Mistakes, 13

Newton, Isaac, 25, 53
Notebook, for data, 18

Oil, 19

Pollution, 19, 52
Presentation, 117–119

Projects
    characteristics of
    light and the
    environment, 78–80
    designing a rocking
    chair, 45–48
    dew point and clouds,
    85–88
    energy in rubber
    bands and strings,
    32–33
    gears, bicycles and
    other things, 28–31
    heating and cooling
    with changes of
    state, 90–92
    keeping heat in with
    insulation, 70–74
    light-emitting diodes
    and transistors,
    98–101
    passive solar-heated
    house, 62–66
    remote sensing,
    108–112
    robots and repetitive
    tasks, 103–108
    solar heating: trapping
    the sun's rays, 66–70
    spinning basketballs,
    34–38
    storing heat from solar
    collectors, 74–78
    string trimmers, 23–27
    tire pressure and
    rolling friction, 20–22
    torque converters and

automatic shifts,
39–45
wave energy, 57–62
windmills, 53–57
wind speed indicators,
92–97

Questions, 12, 16
and science fairs, 117
unanswered, 18

Radon gas, 81
Raft, with paddle wheels,
50
Remote sensing, 108–113
materials and tools,
109
projects, 112–114
Reports, 118–119
Robots and repetitive tasks,
103–108
materials and tools,
106
projects, 108, 113–115
Rocking chairs, 45–48
materials and tools, 45,
47
Rolling friction, 20–23
Rotational energy, 36, 39
Rubber bands and springs,
32–34
materials and tools, 32

Safety, 14
Sails, 50
Science fairs, 116–119
presentation, 117–119

Scientific method, 18
Scientific principles, 12, 13
and judges, 116
Scientists, 11, 16
how they work, 16–18
Solar collectors, 66–70
materials, 67
projects, 69–70
storing the heat, 74–77
Solar food dryer, 82–83
Solar heat
passive, 62–66
projects, 65–66, 69–70
trapping sun's rays,
66–69
Spectroscope, 78, 79
Spinning balls, 34–39
basketballs, 34–38
hoola hoops, 38
superballs, 38
use video to study,
38–39
yo-yo, 38
Springs, 32–34
String trimmers, 23–27
materials and tools,
25–26
projects, 27
Sun and solar heating,
62–70
Superballs, 38
"Survival still," 83

Tire pressure and rolling
friction, 20–23
materials and tools, 21
other projects, 22–23

Torque converters, 39–45
    and automatic shifts,
       39–43
    materials and tools, 40
    projects, 44–45
Transistors, 98–103
    materials and tools, 99
    projects, 101–103

Ultraviolet radiation, 78

Video camera, 38–39

Wave energy, 57–62
    materials and tools, 58
    projects, 61–62
Wave size and wind, 97–98
Weather, 84–98
    change of state,
       90–92

    dew point and clouds,
       85–90
    other projects,
       113–115
    wind speed indicators,
       92–98
Windmills, 53–57
    materials and tools, 55
    projects, 56–57
Wind speed indicators,
    92–98
    materials and tools,
       93
    projects, 97–98
Wind tunnel, 50–51
Work, 19, 28
    working scientifically,
       16–18

Yo-yo, 38

ABOUT THE AUTHOR

Peter H. Goodwin is chairman of the science department at Kent School in Kent, Connecticut. He has published *Engineering Projects for Young Scientists, Physics Projects for Young Scientists, Physics with Computers, Physics Can Be Fun, How Things Work,* and *Practical Physics Labs.* Peter is also a photographer, sailor, and orienteering enthusiast. He built his own home, including a sunroom, where he grows lettuce and other produce year round. He lives with his wife, Susan, and two sons, Hunt and John.